Anything Can Happen

GEORGE AND HELEN PAPASHVILY

St. Martin's Press
New York

Parts of the work appeared originally as short stories in
the magazines *Direction* and *Common Ground*.

Library of Congress Cataloging in Publication Data

Papashvily, George.
  Anything can happen.

  Reprint. Originally published: New York : Harper, 1945.
  1. Papashvily, George.   2. Russian Americans—
Biography.   3. United States—Social life and customs—
1918-1945.   I. Papashvily, Helen Waite.   II. Title.
E184.R9P37   1985   973.91   84-22249

ISBN 0-312-04523-9 (pbk.)

First published in U.S. by Harper & Row Publishers, Inc. in 1945.

10 9 8 7 6 5 4 3 2 1

CONTENTS

For our sister,
MARJORIE WAITE HILL,
with love.

Anything Can Happen

THE FIRST DAY

At five in the morning the engines stopped, and after thirty-seven days the boat was quiet.

We were in America.

I got up and stepped over the other men and looked out the porthole. Water and fog. We were anchoring off an island. I dressed and went on deck.

Now began my troubles. What to do? This was a Greek boat and I was steerage, so of course by the time we were half way out I had spent all my landing money for extra food.

Hassan, the Turk, one of the six who slept in the cabin with me, came up the ladder.

"I told you so," he said as soon as he saw me. "Now we are in America and you have no money to land. They send you home. No money, no going ashore. What a disgrace. In your position, frankly, I would kill myself."

Hassan had been satisfied to starve on black olives and salt cheese all the way from Gibraltar, and he begrudged every skewer of lamb I bribed away from the first-cabin steward.

We went down the gangplank into the big room. Passengers with pictures in their hands was rushing around to match them to a relative. Before their tables the inspectors was busy with long lines of people.

The visitors' door opened and fellow with big pile of caps, striped blue and white cotton caps with visors and a top button, came in. He went first to an old man with a karakul hat near the window, then to a Cossack in the line. At last he came to me.

"Look," he said in Russian, "look at your hat. You want to be a greenhorn all your life? A karakul hat! Do you expect to see anybody in the U.S.A. still with a fur hat? The customs inspector, the doctor, the captain—are they wearing fur hats? Certainly not."

I didn't say anything.

"Look," he said. "I'm sorry for you. I was a greenhorn once myself. I wouldn't want to see anybody make my mistakes. Look, I have caps. See, from such rich striped material. Like wears railroad engineers, and house painters, and coal miners." He spun one around on his finger. "Don't be afraid. It's a cap in real American style. With this cap on your head, they couldn't tell you from a citizen. I'm positively guaranteeing. And I'm trading you this cap even for your old karakul hat. Trading even. You don't have to give me one penny."

Now it is true I bought my karakul *coudie* new for the trip. It was a fine skin, a silver lamb, and in Georgia it would have lasted me a lifetime. Still ——

"I'll tell you," the cap man said. "So you can remember all your life you made money the first hour you were in America, I give you a cap and a dollar besides. Done?"

I took off my *coudie* and put on his cap. It was small and sat well up on my head, but then in America one dresses like an American and it is a satisfaction always to be in the best style. So I got my first dollar.

Ysaacs, a Syrian, sat on the bench and smoked brown paper cigarettes and watched all through the bargain. He was from our cabin, too, and he knew I was worried about the money to show the examiners. But now, as soon as the cap man went on to the next customer, Ysaacs explained a way to get me by the examiners—a good way.

Such a very good way, in fact, that when the inspector looked over my passport and entry permit I was ready.

"Do you have friends meeting you?" he asked me. "Do you have money to support yourself?"

I pulled out a round fat roll of green American money—tens, twenties—a nice thick pile with a rubber band around.

"O.K.," he said. "Go ahead." He stamped my papers.

I got my baggage and took the money roll back again to Ysaacs' friend, Arapouleopolus, the money lender, so he could rent it over again to another man. One dollar was all he charged to use it for each landing. Really a bargain.

On the outer platform I met Zurabeg, an Ossetian, who had been down in steerage, too. But Zurabeg was no greenhorn coming for the first time. Zurabeg was an American citizen with papers to prove it, and a friend of Gospadin Buffalo Bill besides. This Zurabeg came first to America twenty years before as a trick show rider, and later he was boss cook on the road with the Gospadin Buffalo Bill. Every few years, Zurabeg, whenever he saved enough money, went home to find a wife—but so far with no luck.

"Can't land?" he asked me.

"No, I can land," I said, "but I have no money to pay the little boat to carry me to shore." A small boat went chuffing back and forth taking off the discharged passengers. "I try to make up my mind to swim, but if I swim how will I carry my baggage? It would need two trips at least."

"Listen, donkey-head," Zurabeg said, "This is America. The carrying boat is free. It belongs to my government. They take us for nothing. Come on."

So we got to the shore.

And there—the streets, the people, the noise! The faces flashing by—and by again. The screams and chatter and cries. But most of all the motion, back and forth, back and forth, pressing deeper and deeper on my eyeballs.

We walked a few blocks through this before I remembered my landing cards and passport and visas. I took them out and tore them into little pieces and threw them all in an ash can. "They can't prove I'm not a citizen, now," I said. "What we do next?"

"We get jobs," Zurabeg told me. "I show you."

We went to an employment agency. Conveniently, the man spoke Russian. He gave Zurabeg ticket right away to start in Russian restaurant as first cook.

"Now, your friend? What can you do?" he asked me.

"I," I said, "am a worker in decorative leathers particularly specializing in the ornamenting of crop handles according to the traditional designs."

"My God!" the man said. "This is the U.S.A. No horses. Automobiles. What else can you do?"

Fortunately my father was a man of great foresight and I have two trades. His idea was that in the days when a man starves with one, by the other he may eat.

"I am also," I said, "a swordmaker. Short blades or long; daggers with or without chasing; hunting knives, plain or ornamented; tempering, fitting, pointing—" I took my certificate of successful completion of apprenticeship out of my *chemidon*.

"My God! A crop maker—a sword pointer. You

better take him along for a dishwasher," he said to Zurabeg. "They can always use another dishwasher."

We went down into the earth and flew through tunnels in a train. It was like the caves under the Kazbeck where the giant bats sleep, and it smelled even worse.

The restaurant was on a side street and the lady-owner, the *hasaika*, spoke kindly. "I remember you from the tearoom," she said to Zurabeg. "I congratulate myself on getting you. You are excellent on the *piroshkis*, isn't it?"

"On everything, madame," Zurabeg said grandly. "On everything. Buffalo Bill, an old friend of mine, has eaten thirty of my *piroshkis* at a meal. My friend—" he waved toward me—"will be a dishwasher."

I made a bow.

The kitchen was small and hot and fat—like inside of a pig's stomach. Zurabeg unpacked his knives, put on his cap, and, at home at once, started to dice celery.

"You can wash these," the *hasaika* said to me. "At four we have party."

It was a trayful of glasses. And such glasses—thin bubbles that would hardly hold a sip—set on stems. The first one snapped in my hand, the second dissolved, the third to tenth I got washed, the eleventh was already cracked, the twelfth rang once on the pan edge and was silent.

Perhaps I might be there yet, but just as I carried

the first trayful to the service slot, the restaurant cat
ran between my feet.

When I got all the glass swept up, I told Zurabeg,
"Now, we have to eat. It's noon. I watch the customers eat. It makes me hungry. Prepare a *shashlik*
and some cucumbers, and we enjoy our first meal for
good luck in the New World."

"This is a restaurant," Zurabeg said, "not a *duquani*
on the side of the Georgian road where the proprietor
and the house eat with the guests together at one
table. This is a restaurant with very strict organization.
We get to eat when the customers go, and you get
what the customers leave. Try again with the glasses
and remember my reputation. Please."

I found a quart of sour cream and went into the
back alley and ate that and some bread and a jar of
caviar which was very salty—packed for export, no
doubt.

The *hasaika* found me. I stood up. "Please," she
said, "please go on. Eat sour cream. But after, could
you go away? Far away? With no hard feelings. The
glasses—the caviar—it's expensive for me—and at
the same time I don't want to make your friend mad.
I need a good cook. If you could just go away?
Quietly? Just disappear, so to speak? I give you five
dollars."

"I didn't do anything," I said, "so you don't have
to pay me. All in all, a restaurant probably isn't my
fate. You can tell Zurabeg afterward."

She brought my cap and a paper bag. I went down through the alley and into the street. I walked. I walked until my feet took fire in my shoes and my neck ached from looking. I walked for hours. I couldn't even be sure it was the same day. I tried some English on a few men that passed. "What watch?" I said. But they pushed by me so I knew I had it wrong. I tried another man. "How many clock?" He showed me on his wrist. Four-thirty.

A wonderful place. Rapidly, if one applies oneself, one speaks the English.

I came to a park and went in and found a place under a tree and took off my shoes and lay down. I looked in the bag the *hasaika* gave me. A sandwich from bologna and a nickel—to begin in America with.

What to do? While I decided, I slept.

A policeman was waking me up. He spoke. I shook my head I can't understand. Then with hands, with legs, rolling his eyes, turning his head, with motions, with gestures (really he was as good as marionettes I saw once in Tiflis), he showed me to lie on the grass is forbidden. But one is welcome to the seats instead. All free seats in this park. No charge for anybody. What a country.

But I was puzzled. There were iron arm rests every two feet along the benches. How could I distribute myself under them? I tried one leg. Then the other. But when I was under, how could I turn around? Then, whatever way I got in, my chin was always caught by the hoop. While I thought this over, I walked and bought peanuts for my nickel and fed the squirrels.

Lights began to come on in the towers around the park. It was almost dark. I found a sandy patch under a rock on little bluff above the drive. I cut a *shashlik* stick and built a fire of twigs and broiled my bologna over it and ate the bread. It lasted very short. Then I rolled up my coat for a pillow like the days during the war and went to sleep.

I was tired from America and I slept some hours. It must have been almost midnight when the light flashed in my face. I sat up. It was from the head lamp of a touring car choking along on the road below me. While I watched, the engine coughed and died. A man got out. For more than an hour he knocked with tools and opened the hood and closed it again.

Then I slid down the bank. In the war there were airplanes, and of course cars are much the same except, naturally, for the wings. I showed him with my hands and feet and head, like the policeman: "Give me the tools and let me try." He handed them over and sat down on the bench.

I checked the spark plugs and the distributor, the timer and the coils. I looked at the feed line, at the ignition, at the gas. In between, I cranked. I cranked until I cranked my heart out onto the ground. Still the car wouldn't move.

I got mad. I cursed it. I cursed it for a son of a mountain devi. I cursed it for the carriage of the diavels in the cave. I cursed it by the black-horned goat, and when I finished all I knew in Georgian I said it again in Russian to pick up the loose ends. Then I kicked the radiator as hard as I could. The car was old Model T, and it started with a snort that shook the chassis like an aspen.

The man came running up. He was laughing and he shook my hands and talked at me and asked questions. But the policeman's method didn't work. Signs weren't enough. I remembered my dictionary —English-Russian, Russian-English—it went both ways. I took it from my blouse pocket and showed the man. Holding it under the headlights, he thumbed through.

"Work?" he found in English.

I looked at the Russian word beside it and shook my head.

"Home?" he turned to that.

"No," again.

I took the dictionary. "Boat. Today."

"Come home—" he showed me the words—"with me—" he pointed to himself. "Eat. Sleep. Job." It took him quite a time between words. "Job. To-morrow."

"Automobiles?" I said. We have the same word in Georgian.

"Automobiles!" He was pleased we found one word together.

We got in his car, and he took me through miles and miles of streets with houses on both sides of every one of them until we came to his own. We went in and we ate and we drank and ate and drank again. For that, fortunately, you need no words.

Then his wife showed me a room and I went to bed. As I fell asleep, I thought to myself: Well, now, I have lived one whole day in America and—just like they say—America is a country where anything, anything at all can happen.

And in twenty years—about this—I never changed my mind.

II

YES, YOUR HONESTY

Six months in America and already I was a jailbird. Happened this way.

The weeks seemed extra long that first half year I was in New York. No holidays, no feast days, no celebrations to break up the time and then when Saturday came around I had only twelve dollars, at most fourteen dollars in my pay envelope.

The man I met in Central Park on my first day in America gave me a job in his garage like he promised. But after I was there about two months his wife's mother got sick and they closed up and moved to the country. With my poor language, wasn't easy to find another place.

I tried silk mill and after that factory where they made statues—ugly ones—from plaster. I stayed there until head artist gave me camel to cast, only looked like a cow, this camel. I was ashamed to make such a monstrosity animal so I changed shape little bit here and there to give some camel personality to it.

But when artist saw he got mad and told me how many schools he was in—London, Paris, Dresden—(just my point, no camels living in any of those places, certainly) and I'm fired again.

Then I went for house painter but somehow the boss and me didn't suit each other. Finally I met a Georgian, there were only two, three of us in New York this time, who worked in a cleaning factory and he took me for his assistant. It was awful place. I dipped the clothes to take away spots. The gas we used came up in my head and through my throat and out my ears. My every piece of meat whole week long was spiced with that gas.

But no matter how the week went the Sundays were good because then we made all day the holiday and took ourselves in Van Cortlandt Park where there was country and trees and flowers. We could make fires and roast cubed lamb *shashliks* and walk on the grass and forget the factory. For one day anyway we could enjoy to live like human beings.

From six o'clock on, every Sunday morning, subway was packed full. Russians, Syrians, Greeks, Armenians, all kinds of peoples, carrying their grampas and babys and gallon jugs and folding chairs and charcoal sacks and hammocks and samovars and lunch baskets and rugs. Everyone hurrying to their regular place in the park so they could start tea and lay out the lunch, to make the day last a long, long time.

Well, this particular Sunday when all my trouble began was in the late spring. Bright blue day with a high sky and white lamb clouds. The kind of day that's for adventures.

I had my first American-bought suit on and a purple striped tie with a handkerchief to match and a real Yankee Doodle hat from straw. I felt happy and full of prance.

Five or six other fellows and me were visiting around the park. We went from family to family we knew and drank a glass of wine here, tried a piece of cake there, met an uncle just came from Buffalo, saw a new baby first time out and so on.

While we were making shortcut down a quiet path to get on other side of the park we came to a beautiful tree foaming over with white blossoms, how they call in English, dogswood.

"Flowers. Flowers," one Russian fellow, name of Cyrille, said. "I gonna pick. Take bouquet to my lady friend." I don't know who he was, this fellow, he joined us some place we stopped.

"Pick! Pick!" Everybody got the idea. "Pick flowers, take a bouquet to all the lady friends."

"Why spoil a tree?" I said. "Use your brains better. If you want to make friends with a nice young lady, ask her to take a walk. Tell her you gonna show her a bouquet bigger than a house, a bouquet growing right out of the ground. Something interesting. That way you get a chance to be acquainted while you're

walking. Maybe you know so good on the way back
you can invite for ice cream."

No, no, won't listen. They have to break the tree
down. Tear his arms and legs off like wolves. Jumping. Jumping. Who's gonna get the biggest branch?
Makes me sick.

"Personally," I said, "I would be ashamed to give
a lady flowers that I got for nothing. That I stole.
I prefer better to buy. Shows more respect. Or else
don't give."

All of a sudden that fellow, Cyrille, who had
now the biggest bunch climbed down from the top
branches and said to me, "I have to tie my shoelace.
Hold my bouquet for a minute, I'll be back." So I
held. In that minute a policeman was there.

"Awright. Awright," he said. "Defacing public
property. Awright." He asked us our names and
started writing them down on a piece of paper.

"What he does?" I asked Sergei.

"Gives us a summons."

"Summons?"

"We have to go in court."

"We're arrested?"

"Something like that. If we pay the fine, everything
be O.K. But if we ignore, throw away the summons,
they chase us; lock us up."

"What's your name, buddy?" policeman asked me.

I explained the best I can I'm not picking, I'm only
holding for the other fellow.

But he doesn't believe me. "Don't argue," he said. "Don't argue or I'll run you in right now."

I explained again. "Boys will tell you," I said. "I wasn't picking."

No, he doesn't believe them neither. "Don't alibi him," he said.

I'd be sorry to be a man like that policeman, suspicious that everybody is a liar. What's the use for a person to live if he can't thrust nobody?

So he wrote a ticket for me, too, and went away. And still tying his shoe, that fellow Cyrille wasn't back yet.

"This is an awful, awful thing," I said

"It's nothing." Sergei could laugh.

"Nothing! I lived my whole life at home and I was never in trouble. Now I'm six months in America and I'm a crook. Nothing, you think? How my father likes to hear such kind of news? Arrested. What will our village say? The first man from Kobiankari ever comes in the U. S. A.—for what? To go in prison!"

"Look," Sergei said. "You don't even have to go in court. Send the money. Plead guilty."

"But I'm not."

"You only say you are. Saves time."

"Then the policeman's right never to believe anybody. Say first, I didn't. Then, next time, change around, say I did."

"If you won't plead guilty, you'll have to go in court and have a trial."

"Then I'll go."

"Lose a day's pay."

"I lose."

"How about we find the policeman," Arkady suggested, "and try once more?"

"No use," Sergei said. "For myself I'm gonna plead guilty, but the best thing we can do for Giorgi Ivanitch, let's we go back in New York and see a fixer."

"What means vixer?" I said. "Vixer? Kind of a fox, isn't it?"

"*Ef.* Fixer. It's a man. People pays him for fixing things. He knows how to manage all kinds of permits; he fills out income tax blanks; tears up traffic tickets. Suppose you're refused a license for something, you give the Fixer money, he finds some way around to get it anyway for you."

"Still sounds like a fox."

"That's vixen," Sergei said. "Keep straight the words in your head. You get everybody mixed up. Fixers has big connections. Influences."

So we went and Fixer had big rooms to show up he's a Somebody, but the floor was imitation marbles; the stand lamps some kind of cast-metal golded over to look real and on a veneer table sets a big plated vase full with paper roses. Is plank mahogany, the panels in the wall? I felt them. Nope. Plyboard.

"If he matches his office," I told the boys, "he's not even gonna be a real man. Gonna be a dummy stuffed with straw and a victrola in his mouth."

"Shut up or you'll be twice in jail."

"So what can I do for you, my boys?" Fixer came in. "In trouble?"

I showed the summons.

"Trouble with the police?" The Fixer shook his head very sad. "Trouble with the police is serious business. No doubt you're a foreigner?"

"In the U.S.A. I am, yes," I said.

"Well, give me a retaining fee. Ten dollars is customary, but I'll make you for five and we see what we can do."

I paid him the money over.

"Now let's hear."

My committee explained the whole story.

Fixer thought. Looked through his papers. Made a few notes on a pad. Thought again. "I tell you," he said finally, "only one solution. You go in court to-morrow, plead guilty, is about a two dollar fine and it's all over. I use my connections on the side to fix everything for you."

"Look," I told him, "I didn't pick flowers. So I'm not gonna say I did. Hang me in chains but nobody can make me say I did do what I didn't do."

So that ends that. No more help from the Fixer. He's mad.

Sergei suggested how about we go to see old Mr.

Cohen, he was years and years in the U.S.A. Maybe he can think of something.

"Listen," Mr. Cohen said, when we told him everything. "Fixer Mixer leave alone all. Take my advices. I been a citizen for forty-seven years with full papers. President Hayes signed me in personal. Go in court. When they ask you the first question say, 'Not guilty, Your Honor.'"

"Not guilty, Your Honor. What means 'Your Honor'?"

"Means the judge. All judges in U.S.A. named Your Honor."

"Not guilty, Your Honor. Then?"

"Just tell your story nice way."

"With my broken words?"

"Say the best way you can. Probably judge gonna listen and try to understand you. Of course it can happen you get a mean judge, one that's too tired to pay attention, that don't like foreigners to bother him. But very few those kind. If you get such a one, pay your fine, don't argue. But don't be disgusted with the U.S.A. Just come and tell me."

"What you gonna do?"

"Why, next time, I vote against him, naturally. We don't keep him in office no more, if he don't act nice."

So next morning I went in court. Called the other names, Igor, Arkady, Sergei, Philip. Guilty. Guilty. Guilty. All sent money to pay their fines.

Now my name. I couldn't understand a word they asked me. I was nervous. My English was running out of my head like sand through a sieve. How they told me to call a judge? Your Honorable? No. Your Highness? No, that's Russian. Your?— They were asking me something. I had to answer. I took my courage in my two hands and spoke out. "Not guilty, Your Honesty."

Courtroom went wild. Laughing and laughing. Laughing like hyenas. The judge pounded with the hammer. Bang. Bang. Bang! His face was red like a turkey's. What I done? I was sure I was going in Sing Sing and be thrown in the deepest-down dungeon.

But the judge was giving the audience hell first. "Word honesty—applied by this—cause such mirth —contempt of court."

"Young man," Now he was through with them, it be my turn. "Address the Court as Sir."

"Yes, sir."

"Did I understand you to plead not guilty?"

"Yes, sir. Not guilty."

"This officer says you and your friends were violating an ordinance, destroying a tree. Breaking the limbs."

"Yes, sir. Some was picking. I wasn't."

"Have you any proof of this?"

"No, sir. Friends were with me, but they can't

come today. They all pleaded guilty, sent you a fine.
Cheaper than to lose a day's pay."

"Why didn't you do that?"

"Because if I'm guilty I admit it, but if I'm not
guilty, no man gonna make me say I am. Just as much
a lie to say you guilty when you not as to say you
innocent if you did wrong."

"Yes, that's correct. How long are you in the United
States?"

"Six months."

"In court here before?"

"No, sir."

"Ever in trouble at home? Assault or kill a man?"

"Yes, sir."

"How many?"

"Hundreds. After the first year, I never counted
them any more."

"Where was this?"

"In the War. I'm a sniper. It's my job to shoot all
the Germans I see. Sometimes Bulgarians, too, but
mostly they didn't have much interest to show themselves, poor fellows."

"I see. I mean in civil life. When you were not a
soldier, not in the army. Ever hurt or strike anybody?"

"Yes, sir. Once."

"What?"

"Knocked a man's teeths out. Few."

"Why?"

"Catched him giving poisoned meat to my dog to eat."

"Understandable. Only time?'

"Yes, sir."

"Sure?"

"Yes, sir."

"Did you actually see this man," His Honesty asked the policeman, "breaking the tree?"

"No sir. Not exactly, but all the others admitted guilt and he was with them, holding a bunch of flowers."

"I believe he's a truthful man, Officer, and this time you were probably mistaken. Case dismissed."

And then His Honesty, big American judge, leaned over. And what do you think he said to me, ignorant, no speaking language, six months off a boat, greenhorn foreigner? "Young man, I like to shake hands with you."

And in front of that whole court room, he did.

III

THE MAN WITHOUT MANNERS

━━━━━

THE cement in New York got too much for me. Miles and miles of it flattened over the ground and still more heaped up on every side to make buildings. It was like living in a stone vault. I worried, too, that maybe no trees or grass or flowers were left in the world that didn't have a piece of wire fence around them to keep me out.

But where else to go? I didn't have idea. Then one day riding home from work in the subway I heard two men talking. Seems one had just come from a city in the West beyond the far high mountains, a corner of America where forests grow and two great rivers meet, with splashing and crashing, and after like friends go on together. Right away I'm interested. I sharpened my ears to hear more. Seems lots of Slavs were living there with plenty of work, any kind of jobs you want, and high pay for everybody. Sounded very good. I wasn't sorry I had to ride coupla miles past my station before I could catch exact name.

So Saturday, soon I got my pay I went in the railroad station and bought a ticket to this beautiful place. Pittsburgh in Pennsylvania, it was.

When I got there, to tell the truth, it didn't look quite like I expected. But my conscience doesn't let me complain. Served me right for listening to what wasn't my business. Now I have to make the best of it.

So for two months I walked the streets looking for work. Finally I found a job in a glue factory but it only lasted three days. Boss talked so fast I couldn't understand what he wanted. Every night I hurried home to study some more in my word book but impossible ever to catch up with that fellow. He was already a lifetime ahead of me.

So Saturday they gave me pay, six dollars, and told me maybe if sometime I learned better English I could come back and they give me again job. A thin blanket for a cold night.

So back on the street to walk from factory gate to factory gate again. Now in my travels happened I stopped one day in barbershop, Ukranian fellow owned. I wasn't speaking so perfect Russian either this time but better anyway than English and we could talk together. He asked me if I work.

"No."

"Want work?"

"Want eat so naturally I want work."

"Be here tonight nine o'clock. Bring your suitcase. Maybe I get you job."

"What kind?"

"Good job. Be here and you see."

Nine o'clock I was back. Big fellow, rich silk shirt, sat in chair smoking twenty-five cent cigar while two bootblacks shined his shoes.

"Good thing he ain't a octupus," I said to barber in Russian. "Need an army to keep him polished."

"Shut up," he told me Russian back. "Mr. Black," he said in English. "This is the man I told you about. Likes a job."

"Good worker?"

"Yes, sir," barber said, "hard worker."

"Is he O.K.?"

"Yes, sir. Only off a boat a few months."

"Can you speak English?" Mr. Black turned to me.

Now no use to pretend I can, I thought, and lose again another job. Might as well he realizes from first. I shook my head, "No. I can't speak."

"Fine, Fine." Mr. Black rubbed his hands together and looked at me like I'm his Christmas pig and he's ready to carve. "Fine."

Well, shows you never can tell. One place is fine speak English, next time fine not to. That's how it is in America.

"Ask if he's ready to go today," Mr. Black told barber. Barber passed on in Russian.

I shook yes and showed suitcase.

So soon Mr. Black was shaved and squirted all

over cologne we got in his car and started off. Twelve-cylinder Cadillac. Engine sounded like special job.

Here and there we stopped and picked up half a dozen fellows. Two Chinese, one deaf and dumb boy, a Mexican, old German. We were some bunch all right. More for a circus side show.

We rode and rode and rode. Barber said gonna be long trip and he's right. I slept awhile and about daylight I woke up to see smokestacks ahead, big buildings, furnaces flaring up. Mr. Black stopped the car and honked the horn three times. Then he picked up speed and went seventy miles an hour down a hill through an open gate that closed after us.

We got out and they showed us where to wash up. Man brought pot of coffee and some buns and after he took us on our jobs.

Somebody handed me tools. I'm supposed now to be a repairman. O.K. I'm a repairman. I began to work on the machines lying around the shop. A few hours passed. Some man came by, looked over my finished pieces. Nodded his head. Patted my shoulder. That means I'm doing O.K.

This is gonna be a good place, my heart told me. I work hard; study in the nights; take lessons; be early and late on the job; get a promotion. Already I saw myself with a big future, smoking twenty-five cent cigars, wearing rich costumes, only not two men to shine up my shoes. Looks show-off that. Noon whistle caught me just as I was deciding if maybe

Packard car wouldn't be a better investment than the Cadillac.

It was my first day, so, of course, I didn't have any lunch with me. I looked for a canteen some kind to buy a pie, crackers, soda, hamburgers. But I saw the men all passing in file through a door so like the dog's tail I went along behind.

Big, big tables were set out. Thick fried ham slices on platters, bread, potatoes, string beans, corn, butter in pound squares, help yourself how much you want, jelly, pickles. Looked like an Easter party.

But funny bunch of men sitting around, a regular league of nations. Dutchman next to me and on other side some kind of fellow with earrings. Maybe Sicilian. Down the table I saw one man I'm sure is Syrian.

So we ate, after came pie, coffee, ice creams. Whistle blew himself again and we started out. At the door I showed money, I pay for my eat. They didn't take. So I put away. Gonna dock from my wages, I thought. Well is worth it. I'll come every day in here.

Afternoon passed and happened I walked by the fellow I thought was Syrian. It seemed he had duty to burn sheets of tar paper in the furnaces. Funny job, dirty and smoky. I said coupla words to him. He was from Beirut, but a sour kind of fellow. Didn't like to talk. I asked where he lived. Maybe his land-lady will give me room, too?

"Live?" he told me. "What's the matter with you. We sleep in here."

"Inside here? In the factory?"

"Sure."

"Eat supper here, too?"

"Sure."

"Why?"

He wouldn't answer me.

Suppertime came. Two-inch steaks, fried potatoes, peas, carrots, salad, cake, fruits, and after big box of cigars went around.

"Where do rest of men eat?" I asked Syrian fellow as we walked out. I thought maybe if I could find another dining room there might be somebody to pass two words with. Made me sick, this, eating with nobody to talk to.

"What men?"

"Other workers?"

"Aren't others."

"Big factory like this," I said. "You don't mean only us coupla hundred fellows run? Needs thousands or more."

But before he could answer man in charge of dining room motioned me so I followed him. He took me in a big room all full with beds, showed me one is mine. Nicely made up, clean white sheets, good blankets. I laid down and fell asleep to dream what a wonderful country is America. No mistake.

Next day passed. Twice I heard ambulance clang

through the yard; once they unloaded two fellows at the aid station and the other time three, blood all over them. Well, dangerous work, can't be helped. I was lucky to be repairman.

Finally came Saturday and I saw the others wait at a window so I stood with them. Pay day. I got an envelope and inside—My God—forty-two dollars cash money. Nothing out for my eating and sleeping. Company's treat. Seven dollars clear for every single day I worked.

I was so happy I couldn't wait to go in town and spend. I found Syrian fellow. "Want to walk in village?" I asked him. "I buy bottle wine and we enjoy ourself?"

"What's the matter with you?" he said. "Not in your senses?"

Well, I understood. I saw before men, like him. Afraid to drink a glass of my wine for fear he has to buy the second bottle. Crazy after money. I wish him luck he lives to enjoy what he saves, but usually it don't happen.

So I strolled around to look for somebody else. In a club room the company had all fixed up for us I came to two fellows playing *duratchki*. *Duratchki* is Russian card game so I tried to speak a few words with them. Some kind of broken way they answered me. They was Finns or Letts or something. Way I understood from our conversation they learned to speak Russian the year they had their service in the

army and almost they were speaking as bad as me.
Well, not my choice for ideal companions but I in-
vited them in town.

They refused me the same way as the Syrian. "You
without brains. You want to come back, too, in ambulance?"

What's the matter with these people, I thought.
I'm crazy or they're crazy?

"Look, boys," I said. "I ask you a simple question.
Want to go with me, drink bottle wine, my compliments? Or no want to go?"

"They kill you outside." Finn said. "You come
back with no head on."

"Who kills me?"

"Strikers," he answered in English. "Strikers."

"Strikers, all right. But why they strike me?"

"Strikers," he explained, "means who was working
here before and now ain't."

"Why should they be mad at me? They quit. I
came. People changing jobs every day."

"They don't quit for good. They stopped only
because they not satisfied with what the boss gives
them."

"They want the world then. Leave a good job like
this? What do they expect more? Roast beef and free
smokes. Clean beds and seven dollars a day. I be
glad to spend a year here."

"They don't get that. They don't have no eats, no

sleep. Two dollars fifty a day only, they earn. They want three dollars."

"Well costs the boss seven dollars for me," I said. "Why doesn't he give them three dollars. He can't be much of a businessman."

"Big Boss only pays us seven dollars until pretty soon the strikers get tired to wait and come back for two dollars and fifty cents again. Or maybe by that time for only two dollars and twenty-five cents. Then our boss takes us on to the next place."

"On to the next place. Where?"

"Next strike."

"Who's our boss? The man who brought us? Mr. Black?"

"Yes."

This took some thinking over.

They're playing cards again. Smack down ace. Smack down a jack.

"Pardon me interrupt your game," I said after a few minutes, "but do you remember how comes that word in Russian? Strikers?"

"*Zabastovchik.*"

"*Zabastovchik?*" *Zabastovchik.* Yes. And now I remembered. My friend Arsenna. At home. He could read good from the newspapers. He used to tell me all the happenings. Certainly. *Zabastovchik!* "I think I don't like this place," I said. "I'm going away now. But Mr. Black's office, where's that?"

"Main building."

"By storerooms?"

"Next one. Brick."

I went across the yard and up the stairs. Door sign said, KNOCK! I knocked.

"Come in." It was Mr. Black's voice and there he was sitting, his feet up on the desk, a toothpick in his mouth.

"I'm leaving," I said. "But first I want you to give me a paper that says I didn't know I was stealing."

"Oh it's you." He took the toothpick out of his mouth and put it behind his ear. "I thought you couldn't speak English, wise guy."

"This much I'm speaking," I told him. "Give me paper that says I came here by accident. I didn't know I was stealing. Then I'm going. We don't need any argument."

"Smart, huh? You lousy hunkies are all the same. Get ten dollars in your pants pockets and you own the world."

"Hunky. Wise guy. Lousy. Excuse me," I said, "but that isn't talk for a grown man. Write me paper and I'm going."

"Why you square-headed bastard!" He jumped out of his chair. "I won't write you anything. Get out. Get out or I'll throw you out." He pounded his fist on the desk. "Do you hear me? Get out!!"

Inside door to next office opened and tall thin gray man came out. Mr. Black stopped banging and turned to butter. "Yes, sir?" he said, "yes, sir?" Ah ha! This must be the Big Boss.

"What's the meaning of this?" Big Boss spit his words out like they were olive pits. "You know enough to keep your hoodlums down in the yard."

I was getting tired of these names. "Don't call me hoodlum," I said. "I just told your friend, Mr. Black, about that and you're certainly a man that's old enough to know better. Calling names! That's for little kids still with diapers playing in front of their mother's door. You're a man. Act like one."

"Get him out of here."

Mr. Black sat down and started to write me the paper.

"And for your information," now Big Boss was pointing his long finger at me, "I'll personally see you're put on the black list of every plant in the United States."

"Probably millions of people in America never even heard of you," I said. "Worth a pound's weight of nothing to them, your black list. They'll give me a job."

"You'll see about that."

Mr. Black finished writing. "Here's your paper. And when you go out the gate and the strikers beat the guts out of you, don't blame me. You saw the men in the ambulance, do you think that's right?"

"If I steal from a person his wife, his money, his house, his children," I said, "he has a right to stop me how he can. If I steal his job I steal all those things at one time. Naturally he's gonna fight me for it. If he's a man."

"All right. Get out." Big Boss was mad. "One more word and I'll call in the plant guards. They know how to take care of people like you."

"I don't like people to threat me," I told him, "makes it hard for me to go now without looking like I ran away. You take back those words. Then I leave and we call it square."

"You know what those guards could do to you?"

"Kill me? In the war day by day I saw better men than me fall and never get up. Man was born to die. If not today, tomorrow. What difference does it make?"

Mr. Black reached for the telephone. But happened I was expecting this and I got hold of it first. I put on the desk behind me.

"If you want to fight," I said, "I be pleased to fight you any time, any place. Suits me fine right now. But like a man. Guards? What you try to do? Buy yourself courage like a pair of socks. Pay somebody to be brave for you?"

Big Boss's face was purple and his eyelids started to jump. Didn't look like healthy man to me. Probably drank too much to balance what he ate. "You'll be sorry for this," he said.

"Certainly I will," I told him. "I'm sorry already. You think I like to say such sharp words to you, gray-haired, a man old enough to be my father. Of course not. I'm ashamed. But it's your own fault. You disgraced yourself, calling names. Threatening."

Mr. Black whispered to Big Boss.

"No." His mouth was twisting so words could hardly come out. "Let him go through the gates. It's easier that way."

"Good-by." I got to the door. "Can't everybody see the world through the same eyes."

They didn't answer me.

I went back to the club rooms and got a piece of paper and wrote four notes, one each in Turkish, Russian, Persian and Georgian:

Dear Sir:
    Please excuse my mistake. Happened I didn't know I was stealing your job. That's why I'm coming out.
                    Yours very truly,

I signed my name.

I pinned two on each of my lapels, and in my hatband I stood up Mr. Black's letter.

Then I got my suitcase and went through the first gate. After this there was a closed yard about two hundred feet wide. I could hear the men yelling as soon as they saw me start across. "Open," I called to guard in tower at the outside gate. He shook his head and pointed to the crowd. "Open," I said. He released the lock. I took a good breath and went through.

When I came to I was lying on a sofa and some
lady was washing off my head. Four, five men standing around watching.

"We sorry," fellow with one eye said in Slavish.
"Some our boys is too hot-tempered."

"That's O.K.," I said. I moved my head and tried
my arms and legs. "No harm done. What happened?"

"You came out. Was little trouble naturally. Somebody knocked you cold. When you went down and
they saw Black's letter they was gonna kill you
entirely."

"Why?"

"Letter says: 'This introduces my personal repre-
sentative. Please treat him accordingly.' But one of
the fellows said, 'Wait a minute. That scab-monger
Black never told you the truth yet. Why believe him
now? Some catch. See what the other letters say.'
But nobody can read them. So they brought you
here."

Well I told them whole story and we made good
friends. I stayed with this Slavish fellow and his
family until I was better and then I went on the
picketing line, too, with the rest. No smokes; no
steaks; no seven dollars a day there, but no Mr.
Black neither so it balanced out O. K.

Week later the Big Boss decided to finish the
strike. I guess he got tired of paying that Syrian
fellow seven dollars for burning tar paper to pretend
the furnaces were running when he could get men

for three dollars to really fire them. He was a smart businessman after all.

So my friends went back to work and they even got job for me, too, in the repair shop.

But I decided not to take it. To tell the truth I didn't like to work for such a boss—man with no manners at all and is awful thing to say, a man, in my opinion, who couldn't ever learn any.

IV

THE SOUND OF HOME

AFTER this I went in Ambridge and got work in a railroad yard and after that in garage. The months rolled by. I was nearly three years from Tiflis now. Three years. In all that time except for those first few months in New York I never heard one word spoken in my own language—Georgian.

Of course wherever I went and I looked for an Armenian or a Syrian or a Persian—sometimes one of them is speaking little Georgian. But I never had luck.

Once when I was still in Pittsburgh a Turk told me his cousin in Wheeling knew a man who could speak Georgian. So when was my day off—I was still in glue factory this time—I rode over on the bus and found this cousin. But it turned out his friend had been in Batum only a week or two in 1918. He knew the promenade: he knew the fruit vendors, our Keentos—but the language? "Well, naturally, in two weeks ——"

I stayed with them few hours and we ate a little

together, some sausage, some bread, and drank few
glasses wine.

"I know," Turk's cousin said, his name was Aslan,
"I know how it is with you. I went in Indiana State
once for a cook. Six months there, by God, I no talk
to nobody. I don't do it again for thousand dollars.
Cash."

So it went and always and always I was looking
for somebody, anybody who could speak Georgian.
I made it a habit to ask—in the church, in the delica-
tessen, in the Russian Club, all over. Wherever I was.

An Armenian deacon, he heard about it. One night
he came to my room and said, "A Georgian lady is
married with an Armenian. I take you to her and
maybe she can talk with you."

So we went to her house and she *was* a Georgian,
but she couldn't speak with me. She made her
apologies in Russian. Her father and mother had
taken her to Odessa when she was one year old. . . .
"Excuse me, please, but I can't say one word in
Georgian."

Then one day I heard about the big professors at
the university. They were writing books and speaking many languages, and the students came from
everywhere to learn from them. So I thought—
such big professors—maybe one of them can speak
Georgian.

On my day off I took plenty of time and got
dressed up and went over to the university. High up
in a marble building I found two men. Syrian, Rus-

sian, Greek, Persian, Armenian, Tartar, they were speaking all those languages like English—but Georgian, no, not a word.

They shook their heads and one took down a big book from the shelf. He said, "Do you know you speak one of the few tongues in the world that is unrelated to any other language group?"

"Traces of Sumerian may be noted in it, I believe," said the other.

Then they asked me to speak to them in Georgian. But what use was that? To speak without hope of an answer is to beat on a split drumhead. So I shook hands with them and went away.

And after that, when I saw it was hopeless, I began to carry songs around with me in my throat— as some have pocket pieces to touch.

When I walked along or worked on a car, I sang little bits that wouldn't stay out of my head. *"Chongouri sacartveloah. Oh del la del eo."* ("Our Georgia is a singing lute, we are the strings upon it.")

People in the street turned around and the boys in the shop laughed at me, but I couldn't stop. Wherever I was, I sang.

"Alexanderoffskum sadu, musikam igralsa. Rasnim, sortim." (In Alexander Avenue, the music there is playing.")

I was singing that the day I went down to the new laundry for my shirts. "There the music is playing. *Rasnim, sortim——*"

'The lady behind the counter stared when she took the ticket from me, but I was getting used to that.

"You sing in a funny language?"

"Yes, madam," I said.

"My father speaks a funny language, too. A very funny one. He put a piece in the *Sun Telegraph* once. Ten years ago. 'I pay one thousand dollars anybody can speak my language' was what he said. 'Signed Al Monteaux.' A few people came, but nobody spoke it. It's a funny language."

"I guess all languages are funny to those not speaking them, madam. *Nourts Gaprindebe, Nourts Moprindebe.*" ("Fly, butterfly, fly.")

"I call him anyway. Papa! Papa!!"

"*Skals Napoti, harali haralo. Skals Napoti—*" The tunes wouldn't stay out of my mouth.

"Pa——pa!!"

The door of the back office opened and an old man popped out. "*Skals Napoti?* Who sings *Skals Napoti?*" His voice creaked on the song like a dry ox-yoke.

I went toward him. "*Gamarjueba, batano*" ("May yours be the victory in battle, sir.")

And he opened his arms and kissed me, and the tears rolled down his cheeks so fast they almost drowned his answer.

"*Gagemarjos, Shvilo. Madelobtbele wart.*" ("Thank God that the sun rose on this day, my boy.")

"So, at last! I hear my own language again after three years," I said.

His daughter brought him a chair and I sat on the floor beside him.

"Three years," he said in Georgian. "Three years and yet you complain! Think of me, my son. Today I have heard the sound of home for the first time in thirty years."

Then he told me his story. When he was two years old, his mother and his father, a French sea captain, died of fever in the harbor of Batum, and a Georgian family took him home to live with them. And when he was a man he went to sea and finally he came to Pittsburgh in America and here he was ever since.

After that almost every night when my work was through I stopped by the laundry for Papa Monteaux and we bought dry olives and salt cheese and cucumbers and bread and went home to his basement and tapped a barrel. For in all the thirty years when he never heard our language, still he never forgot how to make good wine.

Evening after evening we sat in his cellar doorway under the arbor and sang and told stories and Keento jokes and histories. We took turns reciting "The Man in the Panther's Skin" to each other.

We talked and talked.

We never got tired. The words rolled out from mouths like the Kura River comes down in spring, and our ears were full of hearing.

V

GETTING QUICK RICH

ONE day fellow who worked with me in the garage in Ambridge went on a vacation and when he came back he had a job in Detroit. In Studebaker factory. "And I got job for you, too," he told me.

"I appreciate," I said, "only ——"

"Don't mention."

"Only why I should go in Detroit?"

"Why you should stay here?" he said, "Repairing old wrecks; patching them up when you can go in Detroit and make nice new cars?"

"What's it like, Detroit?"

"Have factorys a mile long. One place they sending a new car off the line every fifty minutes."

"Impossible," I said.

"Well, maybe is fifty new cars every minute. Something like. And there's a big lake with Canada on the other side."

Well, we have a saying that to keep somebody company a Georgian hung himself and I'm no exception. We went to Detroit. I worked at Studebaker and after in the Packard factory. I liked pretty good.

But second winter I was there work began to go slow. I had five hundred dollars saved up so I thought now before I spend all my money away I better put part in something to support myself.

So for a good practical investment I bought two live silver foxes at a fox farm. The idea was the man at farm would keep them there and, like he explained me, when they would have childrens and grand-childrens we could sell them all for furs and make money. I paid for both together $225 for a start and then each week I gave the man coupla dollars for their eating.

So now every Sunday I went to visit my foxes and I got to liking them. The one with gold eyes I named Mellushkella and her husband I called Mr. Fox. I brought them fruits and pretty soon whenever they saw me they were glad in their fox hearts and pushed their long noses through the bars to eat grapes out of my hand.

Only I was coming to see this was slow way to get rich. On the fifth Sunday the man from farm phoned me over. "No use to come any more, buddy," he said, "Yesterday your foxes caught cold and both died."

It was a shock, but after I thought over awhile I saw it happened for the best. Because by now I was liking Mellushkella and Mr. Fox too much and I would be sorry to see them killed or their childrens killed just to hang around a human being's neck.

Now $275 was left. What to do? Better buy propitty, I thought to myself. Propitty doesn't get sick; doesn't die. On holidays you take your friends to see it and when you feel blue you can go and look at your propitty and cheer yourself up.

So from a salesman that came in the Russian Club I bought two lots in Pontiac. He showed us the propitties all on a colored map with names of the owners and names of the streets passing their lots and where gonna be the parks and where the markets. All printed down on map. "From such propitty," he says, "you gonna make little fortune."

Two hundred and fifty dollars was full price. No extras. I paid cash.

Now as soon as I got time I went to Pontiac to see my propitties and first I couldn't find. It was in a big field and I walked through slush that covered over my shoes, but finally I came to my number painted on white stick beside a big hole full with deep mud. And that's my propitty!

In all the world only our water buffalo, Pretty, would like that place. Because she could wallow away half a day in a swamp if nobody whistled a tune to bring her out.

But it wouldn't be practical, I saw that right away, to have Pretty here from Georgia. There are plenty of swamps as good as this one I bought already in Kobiankari and don't cost one penny.

So I went back to Detroit to my room.

Now there lived in that house where I did, altogether on the top floor, me; couple of Egyptian boys, Hassan and Ahmed; one Russian, Vallodia, my friend; a Cossack fellow, Ermak; and a Persian old man, who never would tell us his name.

Ahmed was cooking rice when I came in.

"Give me eat, boys," I said. "Nothing's left in my life. My foxes is dead and buried. My propitty's under water and my money's all gone, only twenty-five dollars." I told them story.

Ermak was sitting in chair reading funny paper out loud to himself in Russian.

"So." He jumped up. "You was cheated. Betrayed. Outraged. Deceived. All right! Ruined. Thinks maybe that agent you're nobody? A man without friends? All alone? We show him. Not so easy to cheat a man when Ermak finds out. Come on, boys. We're going all in Pontiac, this night, and we getting money back, every penny. Money back, or we have his life instead."

"Better don't kill," Ahmed said, stirring the pot furious. "Government in U.S.A. don't like."

"Money or his life," Ermak said. "I don't care which. Let him make own choice. All I know—for me friendship is sacred thing."

The real estate man, when we got there was little

surprised to see us so many, but he was very polite and put seats for all in his office.

"Certainly, boys, certainly," he said. "Might be a little damp, your friend's lot, just at this present time. I don't deny it. But now is winter. Lotsa rain. But in summer when everything dries up who's gonna have a green grass lawn? Who's gonna have flowers as big as cups? Who's gonna have a fish pond with lilies?" He pointed at me. "You, my friend. You gonna have."

"Yes," I said, "But ——"

"Besides," he told me, "gonna be sidewalks pretty soon, next week, and with sidewalks come gutters. Isn't it right? Gutters run water away. Dry up your lot. In six months you gonna double your money for sure."

So he went on and on like a storyteller from Imeretia who has no end to his tale but the start of another. And at last he talked so much Ermak gave him twenty-five dollars, all he had with him, for a deposit on two lots and Vallodia promised to come next day and bring the lady he engaged himself with to talk over buying next door two more lots so he be neighbors to Ermak.

And so we came out and I still had my propitty and it was still under water and still only twenty-five dollars was left.

What to do?

"Let's we be practical," Vallodia said next day. "Think over. In America what's everybody doing all the time? Eating! If they're not eating they're chewing on gum to fool themselves they're eating. Cook some kind of food and sell. Make big money."

But what to cook? We thought and thought. *Piroshkis? Scraporcella,* our nine-layered cake of goat's butter and pounded pistachios? *M'tswade* of deer haunch spitted and broiled? All no good. Finally we decided on *k'hinkali.*

For *k'hinkali* you take fresh bright beef piece, chop fine, cut onions and herbs over; put pepper, little; salt, little more again; water; and mix all. Then you roll a nice dough thin as oak leaf, put the meat in, pinch the edges all around and drop one by one into pot of boiling water and when pot goes plut—plut— plut—plut, it's done. You take out, bite a hole in the end, drink the juice and eat the meat and its coat. Ten, twenty—with good appetite man can eat thirty. That's *k'hinkali.*

The hard part is the dough. Vallodia said he knew how.

"A hundred times I watched my mother to make," he said. "In winter specially my father liked *k'hinkali.* In deep winter when the snow freezes over the top and we could hear the horses' feet crunch through with every step as my brothers came riding home. Then he liked to *k'hinkali,* my father. When it was so cold the church bells from Armavir sounded clear in our village—yes and the voices of the people singing when they passed in sleighs. Flour I need," he said, "and water and egg. That I know."

First time he tried turned to paste. Second time was more like putty; third time, chalk.

"Nothing to do," he said at last, "but ask our landlady."

So Anna Feodorovna showed us how mix and we watched her and it came nice. We wrapped meat, cooked few. Excellent! Almost we ate the whole thing.

Now I packed few dozens in box and went out to sell to restaurants. But every place I stopped they slammed the door and wasn't interested to loan me simple pot of boiling water to prepare a sample.

Finally I came to a Greek who had cooked in Yalta and he was man who understood value of k'hinkali.

He tasted. "O.K.," he said. "I'm gonna take fifty dozen for trial because tonight I have banquet party from Russians. You be here sure six o'clock with k'hinkali. Not one minute late and I pay you cash money. You no fool me. I no fool you."

So I ran home fast as a rabbit jack and my heart was high and bright as the morning clouds on our Kazbeck's Peak.

"We can't ask Anna Feodorovna no more," Vallodia said when I told good news. "So we do this way. Go you on other side of town to the Russian bakery. Explain him our problem. Buy good bag of dough and meantime I employ myself to mix meat. When you coming back we roll dough out and wrap."

The baker understood what I needed. He took a piece the size of a head out of his mixer and wrapped in paper. "Keep in cool place," he said when I paid him, "and you gonna be O.K."

Trolley was crowded and hot like a devi's cook oven. Long before we came even to Dickerson Street I could feel the dough begin to grow under my hands. Man next to me got off and a lady sat down beside. By now dough was size of wineskin. I pushed down in few places and it was quiet for couple minutes. More people climbed in. My dough was breaking through the paper in the corners. No matter how I held still got bigger and bigger and again bigger. My God, I thought, pretty soon it's gonna fill the whole trolley.

The lady next to me acted nervous. Man over the aisle was watching my package with both eyes. It went up little more, almost to watermelon size. I tried to cover with my overcoat.

A woman leaned over from the corner. Her hat feather stuck in my eye.

"You a Russian?" she said.

"No, madame," I begin to explain. "I'm a Georgian. Not the same. Different language, different ——"

"He's a Russian," the woman screamed. "It's a bomb." She pulled the emergency cord.

The trolley was in an uproaring. The conductor pushed back. "Wassa matter?"

Everybody pointed at me.

"Whatch you got there?" he said.

At this time I wasn't speaking English so goodly as I did later but I knew r-o-u-g-h makes English ruff —so d-o-u-g-h must come same.

"I got duff," I said. "Only a bag of bread duff."

Maybe everything still be O.K. but just in that minute the woman opened her mouth and yelled, "Help! HELP! It's crawling on me!"

My dough had broke its paper and was creeping across her dress.

"Please," I said, "please, madame." I got my dough under my arm. "Take. Buy a new dress. Only don't make such a noise. Please." I gave the first bill my hand could find in my pocket. A ten dollar one too. I got to door.

"And stay off the trolleys," the conductor said. "I could have you up for riot."

One thing only, thank God, in the cold air outside, my dough came to his senses and stopped growing. I could carry. But it was almost six miles home and even running part way the clock struck five before I turned into our street.

Now our landlady Anna Feodorovna's father was some kind of a captain or an admiral from the Russian-Japanese War and he had a big brass bell hanging on each floor of the house to remind him of his boat. It was supposed to ring for emergencies, this bell, like somebody falling down stairs and breaking their legs, or electric blowing up, or the bathtub overgoing, or winning the sweepstakes, or something like.

So I rang this bell until almost I busted the rope. Then I leaned over banister. "Come on up! Every-body!" I hollered. "Come on up and help make k'hinkali or we not gonna get finished."

Little lady, Madame Greshkin, music teacher, put head out her door. Luba, Anna Feodorovna's daughter, ran up from basement. The admiral opened his room.

Up they came and we started in. Anna Feodorovna rolled. Vallodia and me, we portioned meat. Luba pinched. Ahmed and Hassan kept new water boiling. Madame Greshkin counted out dozens. "Odin y dva y tree chetireh," like for a song, ONE and two and THREE and four. His Excellency packed. Artash ran up and down and shoved boxes on the truck we borrowed.

Only our Persian, he sat rocking in the far corner with a shawl over his head saying, "My God, My God, is awful thing, this, to happen to man in his old age."

Ten minutes to six we finished. I took to restaurant. Man paid me forty dollars and I came back home.

"Now we figure the profit," Vallodia said. "For meat was ten dollars and for dough three dollars."

"Ten dollars on trolley," I counted.

"And I bought bottle of wine each two dollars for boys, comes four dollars. But can't give no bottle of wine to an admiral from Imperial Russian Navy, so I bought him cognac instead. Six dollars."

"Can't give daughter of admiral no bottle wine neither," I said. "So for Anna Feodorovna and Madame Greshkin, too, roses with sincere compliments. Six dollars again."

"And truck, and gas, and Luba and Artash to movies sit in loge seats ———"

Vallodia thought awhile. "You excuse me now," he said finally. "I gonna speak to you from the heart like a friend and I will tell you these words. You're no man for business Giorgi Ivanitch. You hafta look your luck some other place."

I counted out what was left from my five hundred dollars. One dollar sixty-seven cents cash money.

"Vallodia," I said, "in this case you over one hundred per cent right."

VI

OF ALL FAIR SIGHTS

So I gave up the idea of getting rich and kept on at my job. But somehow the world didn't turn to suit me. It wasn't the money I lost. I didn't care about that. As far as I could see if you don't have money, same time you don't have worries either.

No, it was something else. My days were flat and between the dish and my mouth food turned to sawdust. Even wine lost its pleasure and in my heart lay a cold stone that wouldn't melt. I knew what my sickness was. Loneliness.

True I found Papa Monteaux to speak with and I had a good job I liked in the Packard factory. And by little by I began to make some American friends, men who worked beside me in the shop and they paid me honor to invite me to their homes. In so many things our ways were different, but I liked them. I liked the habit they had of laughing all the time—even at themselves; and the way they snapped the chains of old ideas and dared to try everything, to live and die by their own experience. For me, it was a new kind of bravery.

All this was good but it didn't help the gnawing at my heart. In fact the more American friends I made seemed the lonelier I got. I felt like an ax had chopped my life in two and I missed the part that was left in Georgia. I wanted my new friends but I wanted somebody, too, that I could remember home with. Then I could be a whole man again.

At last one day it seemed I might get my wish. A letter came from Eliko in New York. We call Eliko our Georgian newspaper because he keeps track of all our comings and goings, who marries, who dies, who disappears, who moves. Otherwise so few we are and so scattered we might all be lost from each other. Now Eliko writes me good words:

Greetings and may ever thou be victorious when thou shalt stand in battle before thy enemy. Petro runned into a streetcar. Broke his radiator. Also his arm. Givi is strong big boy going in school. Vasso's daughter got married. One new man came. Says he knows you from Vladikavkaz. He went now to work in Fort Wayne. Close by you? You know him? Name of Uncle John?

Dzea Vanno here in America, in Fort Wayne! I was dancing all around the room to the happy tune my heart was playing.

Of course, I knew him. It almost seems he was in my world from the beginning, like my father and

Dzea Giorgi and Aunt Salome or our Wardo who never came back from the war.

But really Dzea Vanno wasn't my uncle and he wasn't even from our village. I knew him first in Vladikavkaz when I went there ten years old apprenticed to a swordmaker.

It was a dark life in that place. The master made me to sleep in the shop and watch it from thieves and for a bed I laid on flat stone with a buffalo-skin blanket over me.

Work fourteen hours in every day and the master's wife had a pleasure to wash, always to wash. In suds and out of, rubbing and scrubbing, even the walls and windows and street before the door knew her brush and mop. And for all this I had the duty in my spare time to carry buckets of water from the well. Coupla days in that house and a person could enjoy to be dirty rest of his life.

One night the second week I was there I sat outside the back door carving a wooden gun to protect myself if ever the thieves did come and talking to the only friend I had so far, a black dog with one eye, name of Bootsa.

"Bootsa," I was telling him. "What's the use for me? I'm chained by the neck to a mean job. I'm all alone. I have no friends. I'm no better off than you."

Me and Bootsa was thinking awhile. There came a sound from the next yard, but Bootsa snuffled at the gate between so I knew it couldn't be no robber.

"Bootsa," I said, "what I'm living for? Might as well I be dog, too?"

"In that case," voice answered me, "have a bone."

I jumped. In that first minute I thought Bootsa had surely started talking. But it was a man looking over the wall at me. Must he was almost seven feet tall with fierce mustaches and hair black like a devi's. Only his eyes was laughing.

"Have a bone." He pushed me a nice well-done lamb shank. "If you like to be dog, that is. But if you rather be a man, and believe me you gonna enjoy it a lot better. I been a man now fifty years and I'm not sorry yet, why then climb over the fence and eat at the table with me."

So I did and he was right.

Shashliks we had smoking hot and boiled lamb shoulder with herbs and for a side dish meat rolled in grape leaves. And over the fence Bootsa kept us company munching and crunching on the bones we threw him. And then came beef with mushrooms and cream and after that a tray piled high with cakes and fruits and for toasts there were three kinds red wine and two of white. Whatever anybody could want was there. Because this was a restaurant and it belonged to the man who called me. His name was Uncle John.

"My wife, my childrens," he said, "my father, my mother, they're all long dead and in this world I don't have a single relative left so I'm everybody's Uncle John."

Well, I went in Dzea Vanno's cookshop almost every day after that and ran him errands and helped whenever I could find an extra minute. There was plenty to do. Always and always his house was filled with a crowd of poors who somehow catched Dzea's ear with their stories . . . old soldier can't get his pension, coupla fellows runned away from Siberia, widow with five, six kids and no food in her house or maybe a man the czar's police had put a high price on.

But it was Dzea Vanno's own choice that he had more friends than customers. Because if it was money he wanted, he only needed to go for a chef again in Petrograd where princes came to him and grand dukes were happy to pay twenty roubles for a stick of his *shashlik*.

"But, I like better to be my own man," Dzea Vanno always said, "so I came home. Besides life don't pour away so quick here like it does in Petrograd. And with a little restaurant I got excuse to prepare everyday party and enjoy it, too."

Well, this way, that way, somehow time passed and with Dzea Vanno's help I got through my apprenticeship and then was war and when I went back in Vladikavkaz afterward he was gone and finally I came in America.

And now he's here too. I could hardly wait for my next day off. It was on a Tuesday and I took the first train out of the city and I came into Fort Wayne early in the morning. I didn't expect to have any trouble finding Uncle John. He was a cook, so naturally he'll be in some restaurant.

I hired a taxi and I started making the rounds all the restaurants in town. "You have a cook so high so wide looks like this and this." I think I met more cooks that day than most men see in a lifetime but not the right one.

Four o'clock I'm almost ready to give up. "We got six resturants, two clubs, a diner and the hospital left." Taxi man tells me.

"I'm tired of restaurants," I said. "Let's try clubs for variety." He pulled up by a house, private athletic club, brass plate on the door said. A man let me in.

While I'm standing in the hall waiter went past me into the dining room with a steaming platter on his tray.

My search is ended. Because on that dish he carried *Chachobily*, a young chicken simmered in a sauce of herbs and fresh tomatoes until the very bones turn coral. Of all Uncle John's specialties, the best.

I didn't wait longer but I pushed back to the kitchen and there he was. Dzea Vanno. His hair and his mustaches had frosted white and both feet were *chanchulla* from all the meals of good meat and the best wine, but the voice that spoke my name was the same one that called me over the wall a lifetime before, and this man who kissed me now, he was still my friend.

So Uncle John made a table and we sat down to catch up on all the years since our last meeting. And, of course, already Dzea had found somebody that needed his help and I met them, an old Ukranian I think it was this time and an accordion player with the lung sickness.

And the whole club had to come and drink the toast to me that Dzea proposed. "This little glass, gentlemen, for the boy whose life I saved."

"Did you fall overboard? In the war? From robbers?" Everybody asked different.

They didn't believe me when I said, "If no Uncle John today I probably be a dog in Vladikavkaz barking to the moon."

And Dzea was especial pleased when I told him I knew it was him from the *chachobily* went past me in the hall. "Shows," he said, "you don't only love the friend, you recognize the artist."

The accordion player made a song and between his coughings played it for our honor:

Of all fair sights
In this world
The best—yes, ever the best
Is to meet with the face of a friend
In the land of the stranger

That was a fine day such as seldom comes and i was sorry to see the sun set on it.

So I went back to my job and sometimes after that I didn't see Dzea Vanna for a coupla months even a year at a time. Then we would meet for a few days or weeks and again follow different roads. Once we had a whole good summer together in San Francisco. But whenever America would go too fast for me—with movings and different jobs and never twice people's faces, I took pleasure to think about Dzea Vanno, always somewhere, forever the same.

VII

AT THE SUNDOWN IS CALIFORNIA

———

IT's a heart-tearing sight to watch a person sicken and grow thin but oh so worse to see a city die before your eyes. Yet that's what happened to Detroit the winter of 1932. The city, so bright before and full of living, died.

First the factories went and then one by one the little shops, where somebody made his few pennies, closed and left the empty windows staring like dead eyes into deserted streets. The new houses and office buildings stood half finished because everywhere the money was running out like blood draining away.

Came each pay, more and more men found the pink slip that means don't come back again, clipped to their checks. I watched so many, when it was their turn, and saw them pale like men who feel the first chill of typhus. Because it was a kind of typhus, this depression, only the dying was slower.

And why did all this happen? Nobody knew. A stock market in New York? That's what some people thought. But then like others said, "How can a stock market thousands of miles away, never saw me, reach out and take away my piece of bread here in Detroit?"

For my part I didn't know the answer, if there was one. Only it seemed a shame to keep my job longer when men with families needed it, so I quit. With a coupla hundred dollars more I had saved by this time, I started a wrecking business to buy old cars, scrap them and sell the parts and metal for what I could get.

In the house where I lived, things were going bad with them too. Every night when I came in from work Anna Feodorovna sat in her dining room drinking tea, and every night drinking with a longer and longer face.

Friday I stopped to pay my rent. "Be pleased to sit down, Giorgi Ivanitch." She poured a glass of tea for me. "Terrible times. Awful times. Your friend Vallodia lost now his job. And Madame Greshkin, she has no pupils at all."

"Have to expect." I said. "Nobody likes to make music, tra la la, when they hungry."

"Even Ermak and your old Persian gentleman move on Monday. Leaves me this whole big house with only you paying rent. What to do?"

"Maybe times get better," I told her.

"No, I don't expect," she said. "Frankly in my experience they usually get worse. And I thought

America was rich. A place with everything enough."

"It's hard to believe it," I said, "but they can be poor here, too. Like any place else."

Her father, His Excellency, came in and sat down. Anna Feodorovna cut the cake. "Be pleased to take a piece, Giorgi Ivanitch. Today is my father's name day. But who knows if he lives to see another anniversary, my papasha? Or if any of us do. In fact is it any use to struggle more? Often I ask myself. Perhaps to die now is the best thing to do."

"Well," I said, "depends. Maybe you wouldn't enjoy that any better either. Once you tried."

"We have to do something." His Excellency made a big stirring in his tea. "This isn't right how things are going. They promised in America was jobs for everybody, didn't they?"

Why he cares I don't know. He never worked a day in his life. But no use to go into that.

"But what?" Anna Feodorovna asked. "What can we do?"

"Go somewhere else," His Excellency said. "And for that at least I have to admit America is good. No matter where you was already, is always left another place still to go."

"Let it be a place with jobs then, Papasha. Like America was before. And if we go quick, very quick maybe we escape this curse," she crossed herself, "is on Detroit."

"Takes time for deciding," His Excellency said.

"To examine the problem thoroughly." He put his hand over his eyes and started to think.

Luba, Anna Feodorovna's daughter, came in. She was little kid about fifteen, sixteen years old this time with angel blue eyes, pinky cheeks, and curls, yellow as baby duck feathers, all over her head. And to go with all this she had a disposition would fit a pack camel, stubborn, balky, turn a grudge until it was worn sharp, and if screaming didn't bring what she liked to have she wasn't too proud to bite. I was sorry for her brother, Artash, nice little kid, twelve years old. Often I wondered if he would manage to live through it to grow up.

"Hello, Luba," I told. "What did you learn today in school?"

"Don't call me Luba," she stamped her feets. "I told you a hundred times. You're doing it on purpose. Luba! Luba! I have name now of Lucette."

"*Zdravstuite*, Lucette Petrovna," I said. "How you do, Miss Lucette? Glad to know you. Better?"

"Besides I don't go in school more. I quit. I work."

"Doing what?"

"Usher in the movies."

"You leaved school," I said "for a thing like that? How much it pays?"

"I see now every movie, three, four, five, how many times I want, free. That's my pay."

"The theater," Anna Feodorovna said, "Ah, the theater. I can't blame her. Truly she has it from me.

The theater. How I loved. In Petrograd we had a box——"

His Excellency gave a loud cough to show he's caught up on his thinking. "So we agree," he said. "Next thing——"

Artash opened the door and rolled in on his skates, pulled a chair over where Luba can't reach to pinch him and sat down.

"What we agree?" he asked.

"Before I was interrupted," His Excellency said. "I was going to say we agree we're going someplace. Now the mistake we made when we came in U.S.A. was that we chose a place where nobody was speaking our language. So we don't do that again. This time we go where everybody is speaking Russian. We go in Alaska."

"Alaska. That be good," Artash said. He skated over to sideboard to get himself plate. "But who teached the Eskimos?"

"The result of an American education," His Excellency said to Anna Feodorovna. "I hope you're satisfied. My boy," he turned to Artash. "I have the honor to inform you Alaska was a possession of His Late Gracious Majesty Czar Nicolai Alexandrovitch. Naturally everybody there is speaking Russian and take off those skates."

"Czar sold to the U.S.A." I said.

"Gossip. Nothing but gossip."

"To pay his card debts was the way I heard it."

"Lies," he pounded the table. "His Imperial Highness would never have done a thing like that and not told peoples. All lies. So we go in Alaska."

"Yes. Yes." Anna Feodorovna closed her eyes. "To Alaska and the thick quiet snow will fall and fall, frosting over the houses and the churches like little cakes. The bells will ring. And we shall see again the shining faces of our peasants. Yes. We all go."

"But my junk yard," I said. "Why should I throw that away? It brings me a living."

Anna Feodorovna opened her eyes and came back in this world. "Wait, Giorgi Ivanitch. For myself 1 ask nothing. For me a crust bread, a cup of water is enough. But my childrens? You forget my childrens. Surely they deserve a future?"

"I don't deny it. But still I don't want to go in Alaska."

"Pardon." His Excellency interrupted me. "One question. Was you ever in Alaska?"

"Certainly I wasn't."

"Exactly my point. Then how do you know you don't like to go?"

"Besides," Anna Feodorovna said, "to go alone is impossible. A woman, weak, helpless on the road alone with childrens, two little childrens."

Luba cut a slice of *torte* and began to eat.

"Polar bears," Artash said, "and whales. And seals, Giorgi Ivanitch. Seals that clap their hands. I gonna steal a geography book from school tomorrow and bring home to show you."

"But I can see all that for ten cent fare to Belle Isle Park. In the zoo."

"The hand of God rest heavy on the widow." Anna Feodorovna began to cry, her tears spattering down like summer rain. "If you refuse us where I can turn?"

"Don't cry in your glass, Mamasha," Artash patted her hand. "Makes your tea weak. I gonna take you riding on my dog team when we get there. We gonna have dog teams, me and you Giorgi Ivanitch, run like wind." He started to drive the table with his feet. "Mush, Mush. I'm carrying the serum through to Nome. Mush!"

Luba took again cake.

"Gold," His Excellency said. "It jumped my mind entirely, the gold. Any amount of it there once we catch on the places where to look for it."

"Walruses, too," Artash said, "like seals only with mustaches, Giorgi Ivanitch. I know you like."

"O.K. O.K." I said. "Don't cry more please, Anna Feodorovna. I go."

Luba finished last cake on plate and licked her fingers. "Only we not going in Alaska," she said. "I have an intention to be a movie star. So I decided we're going in Hollywood."

This starts a new argument. Alaska or California? But for once I was on Luba's side. If I have to go any place I prefer California. Uncle John had moved there about six months before and he was always writing me to come. Besides from talking to Ameri· cans, I arrived at the conclusion California was a very highly valued place. Anyway there wouldn't be any snow.

And now began preparations for our journey. I went in my scrap yard and put together a car from best parts I had on hand. Was something like station wagon but then again resembled a hearse, too. "But we need truck besides," Anna Feodorovna said immediately I drove my invention home to show it off.

"Why? Goes you, His Excellency, the kids and me. Five will fit good in here with even a place left over."

"But I persuaded Madame Greshkin, she'll enjoy ,he trip," Anna Feodorovna said, "and Ermak thinks he like to come, too."

"But the truck. What's that for?"

"My furniture naturally."

"Anna Feodorovna," I said, "you surely don't mean we're gonna carry your furniture to California? You don't mean that?"

But she did mean.

So finally I found a truck for $150, a pretty good job, one and half ton Ford. We started to load it.

Beds, tables, chairs, carpets—. I didn't say anything but then we had to make a crate for the rubber tree, the rubber tree's going in California, and a fifty pound bag of feathers, too.

"Feathers from the dowry of my own great-grandmother," Anna Feodorovna said. "I have a sacred duty to save them for Luba's trousseau."

"Better Luba finds a husband first," I suggested.

Her only answer was to give me a bird cage to fit in. A big bird cage but the bird died coming from Russia.

"You couldn't leave the cage here I suppose?"

"Please," Anna Feodorovna said. "Why you deny me? So simple my pleasures and so few. Why you make me leave here my bird's cage? Kill in my heart all hope I'll have again some day a sweet canary to sing me songs."

I put it on. Canary's house is all aboard for California, too. And finally after they loaded a harness with bells for a three-horse sleigh and hive of bees Artash kept in the back yard I saw it was hopeless to say any more. Let them do how they want.

"I completed the final plans now for our expedition," his Excellency said one morning at breakfast. He unstrapped his big portfolio and took out a slip of paper. "In the car rides my daughter, the childrens, Madam Greshkin, and Ermak for their protector. And in truck goes me and you, Giorgi Ivanitch. We lead the way."

"We must follow each other and keep together.

That's the main thing," Anna Feodorovna said. "If we be lost, I know we meet only in heaven."

"But how can we manage?" I said. "I can't read maps. When you see it on paper it looks all flat, but when you get there it goes up and down hills and turns corners, crosses over brooks. It never seems same."

"That will be my department," His Excellency promised. "I give the directions. I have a lifetime's experience in travel. I been from Transbaikal to Turkey, from Petrograd to Vladivostok. Don't worry more."

So now was ready everybody for the start?

But no, still Anna Feodorovna needed time to prepare food. For whole next week I smelled baking cookies and the tables were full with stuffed chickens and boiled hams and jars of salad and beets and pickles and whenever you sat had to watch that your sitting was not down on a cake.

"Anna Feodorovna, you make me curious," I said. "What you doing? Maybe you expect to meet Easter on the way someplace?"

"Please, please," Anna Feodorovna had no time. "Don't bother me. It's no joke to pack a lunch for seven people that reaches to California."

"But I expected we'll stop and eat in the restaurants," I said.

His Excellency put his head out the pantry where he was sampling *piroshkis*, that's a kind of crispy little pies filled with chopped meat and hard-boiled eggs. Very easy to eat. "My poor boy," he said, "you really expect to find meals ready for your eating when you stop? That shows you don't have any experience in travel. Maybe in a railroad station, yes, we can buy hot water to make tea. But we're poor people. Who can we send to ride on ahead and order the meals prepared for our coming?"

Well, to argue with His Excellency was like arguing with wind. I kept still.

So at last one day in October, on a bright morning, the air stickling and prickling like champagne bubbles, everything was ready and we began our travels.

Twenty-five, thirty of Anna Feodorovna's lady friends came to say the farewells and most of the men from His Excellency's club and a few boys I knew and a lot of the little kids were in school with Artash and Luba. They all gathered to watch us with round eyes. Truck is packed, gas and oil in the car. Now are we ready to start?

"No," Anna Feodorovna said. "No." She got out of the car. "To go like this. Impossible. To leave our friends with only the memory of a cold house. No. It's too cruel. Let them remember from Anna Feodorovna that she gave with both hands. Let them say she offered on the last day with same heart as on the first day. Unpack the samovar."

So we got it out from underneath the sewing machine and took the spoons out from the sawdust where they was put to don't get scratched and Artash ran to store for a sack of charcoal and Anna Feodorovna laid out most of the lunch to get at cakes. My job was to pass tea and listen to all the ladies tell the details of every trip they took in their lives. And mostly these were trips with very unhappy experiences in them.

By noon everybody finished eating and crying and we washed up the glasses, packed the truck again and this time we're really gone. Good-by! Good-by! Good-by!

Now His Excellency took command. "Turn right; turn left; straight," and got us out on crooked dirt road, one car wide.

"Number Twelve Highway runs out of Detroit," I said. "Why don't we use that?"

"My boy. My boy," His Excellency shook his head. "You'll never learn. Experienced travelers always take the back roads. That way you avoid bandits and hold-uppers. You don't have to pay tolls, either."

So we ride, ride. Sometimes through mud; sometimes across corn fields; we bypassed around cows and detoured through blackberry patches. Night came, we stopped and made a camp in a churchyard. Next morning early we pulled on again. As far as I'm concerned California can't be too soon for me.

By suppertime that second day the lunch was all ate up. Thank God for that. Now we can go in a restaurant like humans. And no matter what His

Excellency thought, I saw restaurants plenty, as many as we left in Detroit, every place we passed through.

So we picked out a nice clean diner and we all went in and sat down at a table and ordered. But my curiosity was itching. How far have we come on our way? So I went up by the front counter.

"Be so kind," I said to the man frying sausage in the window, "to tell me what city I'm in?"

"Youngstown."

"Youngstown? What state is it usually considered to be in, Youngstown?"

"Ohio."

This was Ohio! Terrible shock to me. I'm positive I went through Ohio on my way from Pittsburgh to Detroit. It means we're in exactly the wrong direction.

"You'll excuse me," I said, "if I bother you with one more personal question. In your opinion which way from here would be California?"

He pointed toward the gentlemen's washroom. "West," he said.

I went out that way through the kitchen and into the back yard and sat down on a garbage can. I watched the sky for hour until I got the directions clear in my head from the stars, and then I went back in and ate how they call in English a "blue plate," it means only what is served on it. The plate, naturally, I gave back to the waiter.

Next morning I took charge. "Two days wasted," I said. "Two days that we'll never get back in this world. Spread out the maps. Now Artash you lay a stick down straight to California. O.K. Write me down states it goes across."

Artash put them nicely in order on a piece of paper, Ohio, Indiana, Illinois, Missouri, Kansas, Colorado ——

"Now," I said starting up the truck, "follow me, everybody. Straight ahead. I'm on the right track and where the sun goes down we'll find California waiting."

VIII

SO WIDE AND BEAUTIFUL

―――

AND now for me began one of the best times in my life, day by day I rode along and watched this wide beautiful country open before me. Day by day I found another new coin to add to my bag of gold that was America.

It was so big, this place. Every mile I discovered that all over again. So big. So big. So big. All the wheels in America sang the tune. The automobiles going so whizzing past; the proud motorcycles; the turning tractor treads. Even the locomotives—for a long, long time after they disappeared over the earth's curve, I could hear the rails still humming—So big. So big. So-o-o-o big.

And the people. Wherever we stopped they were glad to make friends and to talk with me. I met Mennonites out of Russia and Bohemians from Prague and Irishmen smelling of good whisky and strong tobaccos off the section gangs, anxious to spend their money, and Welsh slate miners whose voices rose and fell like singing birds. And in little white painted homes in Iowa were what they called "first settlers'" families that was pioneers from Ohio and before that from Vermont and even longer before that?—From England? Now I didn't feel bad about my broken language any more or my stranger ways. I saw everybody is a foreigner. Only difference, some came early and some came late.

I wished I was alone. I could have stayed a week, a month, a year in a hundred places. Only Luba wanted to hurry, hurry so she don't waste a minute to be a movie star, and nothing suited His Excellency: too hot, too cold, too crowded, too lonesome. Anna Feodorovna was weeping, weeping that she ever left Detroit and dropping things and mislaying our travel money that she carried, and every place we stopped she left something behind: her teeth, the silver holder for her tea glass, her special sleeping pillow.

"Personally, Anna Feodorovna," I said—it was the day we had to go from Canton back to Peoria because she forgot her icon hanging in the corner of the tourist cabin—"I don't know how you ever got from Petrograd to Detroit, unless somebody carried you in a bag."

Only Artash had brains to look out the windows and watch America unroll out before us like a carpet from heaven's best weaving.

Illinois, we went through there, riding miles and miles between forests of corn, heavy for harvest; and

Missouri, in a town near the river we ate a kind of American food, fried chicken, in our hands without no forks or plates to interrupt its flavor, and hot golden biscuits, too, so melting good with honey and butter that anywhere else in the world they would have called them cake.

Nebraska I liked extra good because one day just at sundown we stopped at a place to see if we could get some milk. An old, old farmer, he had a beard as long and white as God's, took me out to the barn and he named me his every cow and showed me his big combine, patting its painted side like was a good horse. And what kind of stories he told me! How he walked all the way to Nebraska and lived first in a house made of mud where buffaloes ran in herds past his door.

"Pretty proud I was," he said, "when I got my first team, yep, Dolly and Rachel, and saw my first furrow turn. Yep. And knew," his voice dropped down almost to a whisper, "And knew no plow afore mine ever broke this ground since the world began."

Of course, I saw things I didn't like, too. In this world what place is perfect? But is a cheap kind of loving that can't admit the faults. I saw the poors in sagging houses with funny papers pasted on their walls, and the coloreds pushed away from every table life sets for us others, and the men waiting with such sad patience by the factory gates that didn't need them more. I saw them all.

Before my heart would have broke with this, but now since I traveled America, I was comforted because I knew there was enough for everybody. Only problem was to share it even.

So on we went without trouble until we were about a day into Colorado when His Excellency said he would take the wheel, give me little rest for awhile. So I closed my eyes and as soon as I opened them again, we're miles off the main road, parked at the edge of a river bed. True there was only a trickle of water in it, but the sides were steep and there wasn't any bridge for crossing over.

"The way this happened," His Excellency began, "was ——"

"I don't doubt it," I said, "whatever it was. O.K. Ermak, you got the lightest car. I'll pull around and you go first. If you get across, I'll come after."

"If I get stuck?" Ermak said.

"Still be easier to pull you out than me."

"No. No. You go this way. I go that way——" Ermak is the kind of man the minute you say black, he has to say white. "If I go here ——"

"No time for the philosophy of crossing rivers," I said. "Be dark pretty soon. If you won't go, I have to." So I started over. Of course, in the center I got stuck, and immediately my wheels started to disappear in the sand. I was sinking.

"My furnitures. Help!" Anna Feodorovna stood

on the bank and wrung her hands to the sky. "Help! They're going!"

Truck sagged another inch.

"Don't worry, Anna Feodorovna," I got out and looked at my axle. I was so mad I could chew on knives. "Don't worry. Only a matter of time until I come out in China. I deliver your furnitures back in Vladivostok."

Everybody screamed and they came out and started carrying off the things, one by one, up on the far bank. Truck stopped settling then, but I still couldn't move it. I got out and went downstream to see if I could find some pieces of wood. In the distance I saw a lot of men coming towards us with horses and wagons and so much dust it must be they were moving sheep. I went out to meet them.

"Give me hand, Boys," I said. "I'm stuck in the river."

But it seemed they didn't understand me. They made Ho-Ho-How-How among themselves and finally one young fellow rode up from the back and asked me in English what I wanted.

"What nationality you folks are anyway?" I asked him. "I'm stuck in the mud. Maybe you can help me?"

"We're Navahos. Wait. I ask and see what we can do."

"Nava Whos?"

"Nava Hoes. Indians."

"Glad to meet you," I said. "I often heard about you fellows, but I never expected to have the good luck to see."

So he rode to the back and talked with an old man. Meantime I told my party, "It's Indians."

Anna Feodorovna went on her knees, crossed herself, and started to pray out loud. His Excellency jumped off the unpacked sofa where he's resting and started throwing fire tongs and walking canes and pokers around like a crazy man. "Where's my sword? My sword! My sword!"

Ermak turned the kitchen table over, piled the chairs up, and crouched down behind it. "Don't be afraid," he said to Madame Greshkin, "before I die I try to shoot you and Luba, too, but if God wills overwise—" he opened a drawer in his barricade and pulled out a butcher knife, "use this, but don't ever let them take you alive."

"Shut up," Luba said. She tipped the mirror in the bureau, patted her curls in place, and put on a second coat of face. "Come on, Artash," she took his hand. "Sister's gonna take you to see the Indians."

"I take myself," Artash said. "Let go my arm."

Meantime Indian came back. "All right," he said. He waved his arms and the rest followed after him, and they drove their horses and wagons down into the water.

"Hi-ya. Hi."

"Hi," another one yells. And one, two, three, truck was out, and next they pulled the car across.

"I guess you're like a village," I said to young Indian when all this was over, "so I like to meet your headman."

He took me to an old Indian that made me Ow-Ow-Ow sounds. I don't know what it meant but for politeness I did the same back to him. We was sitting quiet for a few minutes after that, both of us figuring out, I guess, what kind of man the other was. Finally I asked the young fellow how much they wanted for their work.

They talked some more together and at last he said, "Nothing."

I expected maybe it was gonna happen like this, so I prepared myself on the way over to them. I had a five dollar bill ready, and so it doesn't look like pay, I wrapped it up in a nice red silk handkerchief I had.

I offered it to the old Indian. He looked over the money and the handkerchief on every side, and then he said something and pretty soon another Indian brought a good belt up and handed it to me. Few minutes more passed and then the young Indian came back and gave me a five dollar gold piece.

So now it looked like we were good friends.

I asked the young Indian if he would sell me a sheep. After some more talk they brought one up.

"Now," I told them, "I'd like to invite all you boys

to a party. I cook you a sheep how we do it in my country. Agreeable?"

I killed and skinned and cleaned it, and then I cut broiling sticks, and Artash and two little Indian kids built me fire, and I made *shashlik*.

They're funny people, Indians. Soon I started to make my way they killed another sheep and cooked too. Only different from me.

After about two hours passed, it was all ready. I called my party, but they wouldn't come.

"Certainly not," Anna Feodorovna said, "my chil drens might catch something from them. Look at their clothes."

"No, no," His Excellency had found his sword and buckled it on. "No, Ermak and me stay on guard here. For your own protection, Giorgi Ivanitch. They might turn on you any time."

Luba wouldn't even answer me. She was sulking in a corner like a cat got its tail stepped on.

So only Artash came along. I started with old headman and passed a good smoking hot stickful of meat to everyone, about twenty or twenty-five of them altogether in the order what I guessed their ages was.

I don't know if they liked it or not, but anyway they was eating with loud sounds.

When we were all finished the young Indian, the one does all my talking for me, came up. He said, "My grandfather likes the way you kill sheep and clean and cook. He wants to know what tribe you come from. How many sheep you have? Is good hunting there?"

"I'm Georgian," I said, "from the other side of the world. In our village was about two hundred sheep last time I knew. If we kill with care, our hunting is enough for all."

Young Indian gave me a little piece of thing from stone, and I didn't have much left except a combination corkscrew knife so I made him present of that. We shaked hands, and they all rode away.

"I think they the most filthy disgusting people in the world," Anna Feodorovna said. "They smell." We got the furniture all loaded on and were ready to start off again.

"And ugly, too," Luba said. "Hideous."

"They're savages," His Excellency said, packing his sword back in the umbrella stand. "Can't expect more. Wild savages."

"Served you right, all of you, if they left you in the river," I said. "For my part I think they knew how to act like men, and they did."

IX

IT'S CALIFORNIA

BEING stuck in the river bed didn't do my truck any good, but I went limping across Colorado and down through Arizona trying to keep up with them in the other car.

My two rear wheels were giving me trouble. The old hard rubber tires started to spin loose and I patched them up best I could but it meant I had to stop so often the others were getting restless. So finally they decided they better go on ahead and we meet all in Cailfornia.

When we started the trip we each put thirty dollars travel money in the pot and Anna Feodorovna kept this in her charge and from it she was gonna pay for gas and our sleeping and what food we bought and the postcards and so on.

Now if we separate we have to divide up our cash. Anna Feodorovna opened her purse. Well! Nobody is more surprised than her to find only $8.75 left.

"My God," Ermak said, "What happened to the rest?" We all listening to hear the answer to this.

Anna Feodorovna looked through everything again. Shook the lining, emptied her cardcase; thumbed through her papers. "I know," she said at last. "I know exactly what happened. I spent it." She started to cry. "I'm a thief."

"Stop crying," I said, "Can't do anything now. Scrape your pockets, everybody, and let's see how we stand."

Ermak turned his inside out. Empty. Artash had three dollars he was saving this long time to buy an automobile. Madame Greshkin asked us if we please be so kind to all get out of the car. We did and she pulled down the window shades. We stood on the road. Five, ten minutes passed. At last she snapped up the curtains, opened the door and gave us a five dollar bill. His Excellency added $1.25 to that. If Luba had anything she didn't tell. Now put all together with fifteen dollars I had, we got thirty-three dollars exactly and California still six hundred miles away.

After a lot of talk they decided they take twenty-five dollars and go all in the car to Hollywood. I keep the other eight dollars and try to get to Yuma.

"You wait there," His Excellency said, "and inquire at the post office and in a coupla days we send you the money to come the rest of the way."

"Where you expect to get it from?"

"I have a nephew, my sister's oldest son, he came through Siberia to Los Angeles. He lends me."

"You know where he lives?"

"Certainly I know. He's my nephew, isn't he?"

"I make one more suggestion," I said. "And after that I save my words and sell to a dictionary. Let's go in the next town and whatever they offer for truck and furnitures we take it and go all in California."

Anna Feodorovna was in tears again. It was like talking to a wet sponge.

"All right," I said. "All right." So they take their suitcases and off they go. "And be sure you call at the general delivery in Yuma," His Excellency hollered out the back, last thing, "for your money."

I drove on past Gila Bend, past Sentinel, and even with no money, living on chile beans and soda crackers I liked this part of the trip.

Soon as the sun went down I made a camp beside my truck and cooked whatever I had. Sometimes I talked to the men passing on the road. Sad men carrying blanket rolls like humps on their backs. That wouldn't be a life for me, I decided as I watched them walking, walking, walking. Walking to nowhere. If you're not father or husband, son or brother; neighbor or friend to somebody, who are you then to yourself?

And after in a minute night would come and the colors of the desert fade until nothing was left except maybe from a far-off cabin a lonesome light would poke a hole in the dark.

Best of all I liked when I could stop near tracks
and all through the night wake up to see the trains
go flashing back and forth like threaded needles lac-
ing America together. No wonder in this country
they save their most beautiful names to paint on the
freight cars: the Atchison, Topeka and Santa Fe;
the Delaware Lackawanna, Route of Rockets, Detroit
and Mackinac, Huttig, Mansfield and Nacogdoches,
Black Diamond and Nickel Plate.

So on I went and about ten miles outside Yuma
just when I'm congratulating myself everything gonna
be O.K. my right rear tire whipped off and curled
and uncurled itself across the sand like a big snake.

One look and I knew that was finished. I sat and
waited almost the whole afternoon for somebody to
pass and give me a lift into town. Not a single car.
Then I tried to see if I could make it on the rim. Mile
of that and I was riding on a square wheel.

So I pulled over and made myself comfortable.
Looked like this be my home for some time. Next
morning I managed to get into Yuma. No letter so I
shopped around in all the junk yards and at last I
found a good Ford wheel—but for $10. I had $4.50.
I waited for afternoon mail. Again nothing.

Back to my truck. Next day I went after my letter
again. Not yet. So almost a week passed this way and
once every day, as least, I went in town and I got to
know that road and every bush and cow skulleton

and tin can and old piece of wreck beside it like the inside of my own hand.

And at last one morning I went in the post office, man knew me by now. "Here's your letter," he said.

But it wasn't a letter. It was a post card. Picture of palm trees on one side, "Main Street looking east" the printing said. I don't care which direction he looks. I turned over. His Excellency's hand. "We come in here O.K. Thanks be to God. Weather is fine. We was twice on the beach. Artash saw a movie star in the fish market." Few more lines. Gave their address. Down at bottom was P.S., "I didn't find my nephew yet, but don't worry. I keep looking."

I went out on the steps of the post office and sat down to think. Finally I made up my mind what I'm going to do. I went back in the junk yard. Will he give me Ford wheel for four dollars cash and I send him the rest? No. For four dollars cash and my camera? No. Four dollars cash, my camera and my cuff links? No.

"I guess it wouldn't be any use to throw my head in either then," I said.

I went out. At the gate I stopped. "How much for this?" I asked him. It was an old Nash wheel lying in the grass...but all of a sudden it gave me idea.

"A dollar and stay out of my yard."

So I paid him and I started off rolling my wheel ahead of me. About mile out of town a car stopped and an American fellow gave me a lift. He didn't say nothing to me so I did the same to him until he came near the bend and then I asked him if he minded to stop a minute I want to pick up an old wreck battery I saw lying there. He pulled up. "Are you a junkman?" he said.

"No," I told him. "My car, Ford truck, broke down and I lost my wheel and I'm going to put this wheel on instead."

He turned and looked back at it. "That's a Nash wheel," he said, "Somebody stung you."

"I know is a Nash wheel, but I'm gonna use anyway."

"Won't fit."

"I make fit."

"Can't."

"I can try." Just then I remembered something about Americans. This is gonna get me to California, I thought to myself. "Sure I can," I said out loud. "I know I can. I bet you twenty bucks I put on and my truck runs."

We was up to my truck now. I had all the furniture unloaded off and the frame braced with some wood. He got out and looked it all over. "Twenty bucks it don't run." He sat down on the running board to watch me what I'm gonna do next.

I gathered twigs and started a fire with scraps of paper on a piece of old tin and when it got going good I threw the battery on. Meantime I raised my truck a little higher with the jack and took the wheel off.

I tried the Nash wheel on the Ford hub. Fitted pretty loose. By this time man got so interested he was gathering brushes to keep the battery burning. Finally the lead I wanted melted out from the battery on to the tin and I poured a little into the wheel and hub joint and filled up the holes and worked it into shape until it fitted good. Then I put the wheel on and drove a few hundred feet. Everything O.K. Only my truck looked now like he came back from the wars with one leg shorter than the other.

"Son of a gun!" man said. "I never believed it if I didn't see. Lucky thing for you that you remembered that old battery."

"No," I said "the lucky thing was I remembered Americans always ready to bet on anything."

He peeled off two ten dollar bills. "You win. But you're wasting your time on automobiles." He got in his car. "Try the horses."

I was thinking over that while I loaded the furnitures on again. Some kind of joke he meant, because even I know is impossible to change horses legs around. If they break one, have to shoot.

So I'm back in Yuma with twenty dollars cash and I buy the Ford wheel and put on, eat a nice supper, and I'm ready to start.

So I rode along. I didn't have too much money, but I ate slim and I managed. The last night I was almost there so I decided not to sleep but just keep going and about midnight I pulled into Los Angeles.

I found address His Excellency wrote me, but they
weren't living there any more. "No," landlady said,
"They moved all in Hollywood." She gave me another address.

I kept going. All kinds of curved streets and up
and down roads, but at last I came to place. I rang
and rang until I woke them up and they all came
tumbling down the stairs, His Excellency still in his
nightcap with the red tassel.

They turned on the lights. Quite a place they
rented. Sofa made out of pipes and blue leather chairs
and glass tables. Looked like good, dollar-a-haircut
barber shop.

"Well, here is I am," I said. "I thought I never
make it. I went—" Luba came trailing down the
stairs in some kind of thing made out of pink fur,
be interesting to see the animal that fur came off of—
"And now, Anna Feodorovna," I finished my story,
"you're worries are over. We unload the furnitures
right now and you can tell us where to put it."

"Put it?" Luba said. "What we care where you
put it, that old junk. We bought this. Put it in the
scrap heap." She turned up her nose like a bulldog.
"I'm in the movies now."

x

HOW CHANCHO SOLD MY NOSE

IN HOLLYWOOD there wasn't much choice of jobs that time except to be in the movies. So I went in the casting office and the next thing I'm in the movies, too. But always they called me to play Cossacks. No variety.

One day, I forget if I was turning back the hordes of Genghis Khan that time or was I being mean to the Volga boatmen again, well anyway, I got disgusted. I said to myself: If you wanted to ride a horse all day and wear a *cherkesska* and a fur hat you could have stayed home in Kobiankari. No, you came in America for something different. Better you look to find that something.

So I went to San Francisco and I looked for a job there. But before I had a chance to find one, about the third or fourth day I was there, early in the morning came a knocking on my door and Uncle John rushed in from his room across the hall.

"Wake up! Wake up! Bijo!" He was puffing like

93

an upgrade train and in just as big a hurry too. "I have to be in Calistoga eleven o'clock. They gonna cut Boris up."

"Who is?"

"Some doctors. Meantime until I come back I make you a present of my lunch business."

"Lunch business?" I said. "I want lunch business like I want a hole through my head. Give it to somebody else. I want to work on an idea I have for an oil gauge on cars."

"No. No." He pulled the keys off his ring. "I got full trust in you and you won't have any trouble. Chancho is there to help you out whatever you need. Good-by." He's halfway down the stairs before he climbed back up and put his head in the door again. "A thousand sandwiches before noon," he said.

Was unluckier man than me ever born? If there was, he didn't trouble himself to grow up.

Now to explain the idea of this business—Uncle John prepared lunches in boxes to sell to men who worked too far from a restaurant or maybe didn't get any time at all at noon but had to eat right on their job.

And because Uncle John was a clever buyer and knew how to pinch apples like they were pretty girls and always talked an extra pickle to the dozen out of the dealers he made four, five cents profit on every lunch he packed.

After he got these lunches ready two salesman,

Russian fellows, came and took out in their cars and carried them around on a regular route to factories and garages and construction jobs, any place they could sell them, and they made six, seven cents commission on each box.

And the men that bought them got two sandwiches, an apple, a piece of pie, a pickle, maybe a hard-boiled egg, cupcakes, sometimes candy bar or few peanuts—all for a quarter. So everybody was happy—except me who had now to make the sandwiches, a thing I despised. No eating at all to a sandwich from my point of view.

When I went in Dzea's shop I found Chancho sleeping on the empty pie carriers with a case of mayonnaise for his pillow. He was a simple-minded fellow, this Chancho, that Uncle John found starving down on the *embarcadero*. I don't think he knew himself who he was or where he came from. Certainly nobody else but Dzea would ever give him job, I'm sure of that.

"Chancho." I gave him shake. "Let's get started. What Uncle John makes first?"

Chancho woke up looked all around room and finally got an answer for me off the ceiling. "Sangwikshes. Tumor and salmon."

"Bring me how many cans of each we need."

"Only one kind of cans." He almost split his face open with a grin. "Everything comes out of same can."

Out of same can! Poor Chancho. Really simple. "O.K. You make." That was simpler than arguing with him. "What next?"

"Easter eggs."

This was now the month of July so I understand he meant by that hard-boiled. While I prepared, I watched him what he's doing. He opened the salmon and separated it nice; in one dish he sorted the bones and skin and the dark pieces and mashed it up. "Salmon salad," he said to me. In the other bowl he put the light part of the fish was left and mixed this with mayonnaise. "Tumor fish." He's laughing happy as a horse in spring pasture. "You never expected, did you?" he said.

A butcher came in piled high with liverwurst and salamis and sausages. "Today is our day we take fresh ham," Chancho told me.

"What do we make that into," I asked him, "stuffed turkey?" and as it turned out I'm not far wrong. First we used it for roast pork sandwiches and what can't be sliced straight was mixed with chile for the barbecue special and last of all the scraps were chopped with celery for chicken salad.

For my part people who eat sandwiches deserves to be fooled and I guess they usually are.

So the days passed and Chancho and me were working along fine together getting the lunches out O.K. I got so I can deal out bread like cards, trump with piece of meat, whip butter over the top slice, slap it down and there's a sandwich. In fact only one trouble. No profit showed.

This made me feel ashamed. Here Uncle John trusted me with his business and put full confidence in me and I can't return him any dividend. Finally I drew twenty dollars out of my savings and sent it up to him.

Most of this was Chancho's fault, not that he's crook—no honester fellow ever lived—only he believed whatever people told him and it ran into money.

A salesman came with a new health product at twenty cents a pound that took the place of salt he said. Naturally Chancho wanted all our customers to be healthy so he took fifty pounds.

When I came home I was mad. "Chancho," I said, "plain salt was good enough for your father and your grandfather, besides it only costs a quarter as much."

Chancho felt so bad he went into the kitchen and made a cake with pink frosting for me and squeezed letters on that said *"Greetings and Long Life to Giorgi Ivanitch.* So how could I stay mad—until the next time when he bought two cases of red and yellow and purple and green colored cocktail toothpicks to put in the lunch boxes.

"Cheers our customers up," he said, "more than plain white."

So I began to hide the money away from him but

still after everything was paid there wasn't much left.

What we really needed was more customers so I went out myself to see if I could build a route. Here and there I did pick up some, eight fellows in a sewer excavation, ten girls at the laundry, fifteen men on a construction job, and at the National Guards rifle range they liked our sample so well they gave me a weekly order for three hundred sandwiches and one hundred and fifty milks.

But still it wasn't enough and at last I had to write Dzea the truth.

He sent us a letter and said, "I can't come home. Boris is still sick and needs me here. Better you sell the business for what you can get. And don't worry, my boy, another business I can always find but not a friend like Boris."

So I tried an ad in the Russian paper but who wanted to buy a broken-down business? A few people came and looked over our equipment and wrinkled up their faces because the slicer isn't automatic and the icebox leaks. Finally one couple, Mr. and Mrs. Marinoff, offered us five hundred dollars. I wasn't there but Chancho told me when I came back from my route—back with half my boxes unsold. Total loss.

"Man and lady was here. Give five hundred dollars," he said. "But Uncle John needs more money than that to live on until he starts new business. So I don't take."

"You don't take," I hollered at him. "We be lucky to get three hundred dollars. Where they live?"

But he didn't know. I was so disgusted I liked to lock the door and throw the key in the bay. By the next day though I was glad I didn't because all of a sudden my lunch boxes sold better. Seemed everybody was buying from me. Now it was the other lunchmen's turn to watch with green eyes.

Second day I was even more popular. "Give me three boxes, lunchman," one fellow said.

"You got a big appetite," I told.

He laughed like anything. Next fellow said, "Pick me out good one, lunchman."

"All good," I said, "double cheese in every sandwich."

He winked me eye. "You bet," he said, "you bet."

I had to go back for fifty more boxes. I found Chancho talking to two people and it turned out these were the ones that wanted to buy for five hundred dollars, but my business was so good maybe Chancho was right. We needed more. They offered five hundred dollars again. I didn't say yes and I didn't say no. I went on back where we kept our supplies to pack my extras.

"Who's he?" I heard through the partition the man was asking Chancho.

"The boss."

"Well, he's as ugly as sin anyway," the lady laughed. "Got a nose lie a parrot."

"You go away now," Chancho told them. "I have to pack the afternoon boxes. Go away." Poor Chancho, I could tell from his voice he's mad because they insulted me.

"I give you $550," the man said, "and you can keep fifty for yourself."

"Go away."

I came out.

"I tell you," Mr. Marinoff said to me, "let me ride on your route once with you so I see what you're selling. Maybe tomorrow morning?"

I didn't have any objections.

Meantime our business was getting so heavy I needed extra money for supplies. I had hidden fifty dollars, the last penny of my own money from the bank that I was saving for a positive emergency, and this seems to be it.

"Chancho," I said, "we're going so good I'm gonna try one thousand lunches extra tomorrow. Easy I could have sold today."

But when I went to get my money out of its safe-keeping place, it was gone.

"Chancho," I said, "did you find fifty dollars in the flour bin?"

"Yes," he gave me happy smile, "$51.50 altogether."

"What you done with it?"

"I put back in the business."

"For what?"

"Here and there," he said, "I put back."

Health salt, toothpicks—what now? "What you bought? Show me. Maybe I can sell it. Get something."

No, can't get two words straight out of him. He put back in the business. How much? For what? He couldn't tell, he counted on his fingers frontways and back again, and got the same answer. He made such sad dog eyes at me I finally say, "Forget it, Chancho."

Well, he's how God made him. Can't help it I suppose, and I went out to take a walk around block before I exploded.

When I came back Chancho had everything ready someway. He had talked meat out of the butcher and thirty dollars cash money beside and at five-thirty next morning I was ready to start out with all my extra boxes when this Mr. Marinoff who wants to buy business shows up to ride with me. O.K. I let him come.

At the first gate the boys almost mobbed me for boxes. Next place they were standing in line waiting. "How happens you so popular?" Mr. Marinoff said.

"I don't know myself," I said, "except I never skimped on my boxes and although we got a little fancier names for some things than I like, still I sell honest food and I guess everybody came to find it out."

"Four boxes, lunchman."

"Six boxes!"

"Don't forget me, lunchman."

"Save me three," foreman was hollering from the back.

So now Mr. Marinoff saw this kind of business his eyes started to shine and he sharpened his teeth like a wolf. "Well, well, well," he said, "I didn't know you had this kind of a business."

I didn't know it myself but I didn't explain. When we got back in the shop his wife was waiting for him and they talked in a corner.

"All right," he said finally, "forget everything that happened before. We offer you eight hundred dollars cash money." He opened his wallet and thumbed the bills so they made a rich crackling.

But I'm not a fish to be catched with that worm.

"No, we're not interested," I say.

Poor Chancho he's anxious now to make up for all the trouble he's caused me wasting my money. He shook his head like the wigwag signal on a railroad crossing. "No, we not interested."

"What do you want?"

"More than that," I said.

"More than that," Chancho echoed.

"Nine hundred?"

"Thousand dollars cash right now," I said.

"Right now," Chancho said. "Right now."

But they can't come to that and when they found they couldn't pound us down they went out.

So now I had to go to the fruit market. With all these lunches it was gonna take plenty of time to buy. "Only Chancho," I said as I was going out, "for God's sake sit in chair and whatever you think of don't do it, please, until I come back."

I got two boxes of apples and basket of oranges and picked out some plums and in less than half an hour I was back in the shop. Chancho still sat in the chair. Only now a pile of bills was stacked up in front of him.

"They came back," he said, "and I sold the business. I sold it sitting right here in chair, Giorgi Ivanitch. I never moved. Uncle John gonna be glad. Gonna be glad." He clapped his hands, poor fellow.

"I hope," I said. "But let me count the money first. Twelve hundred dollars. He'll be plenty glad. But what's the extra for?"

"They came back," Chancho said, "and offered me a thousand but I told no. Thousand was for twelve o'clock. I told them Giorgi Ivanitch said, 'Thousand dollars, right now.' That means twelve o'clock. Since then the price went to twelve hundred."

"And?"

"And lady hollered at me and man had sour face, but I sat in the chair and finally they gave me twelve hundred dollars."

"What was two hundred dollars for?"

"Your nose, Giorgi Ivanitch, because that lady insulted your nose."

"Thank you, Chancho," I said, "I be proud to sell my whole face for that price."

So in a few hours, as soon as Mr. Marinoff took possession, Chancho and me caught the train to Calistoga and of course Uncle John was delighted to see us. We gave him the money and for three days we was eating and drinking and singing and having a good time—even Boris who was out of the hospital. All day long the house was full of Dzea's friends who heard the story and came to see the nose that brought two hundreds dollars cash money.

"Now," Dzea said when our holiday was all over, "I decided I'm gonna buy a hot springs bath resort here and you can be my partner and Chancho is our assistant. How that suits you?"

"No, Dzea," I said, " I stay a little while longer but then the time is come for me to go."

"Well, anyway," Dzea said, "I want you and Chancho to buy yourselves little present." He gave us each two hundred dollars.

So I picked out material and had my first tailor suit made to order. Dark gray it was with such a cut to the shoulder and a drape to trousers that when I wore it nobody could tell I'm not a born American. And the proof it was a good investment, I'm still wearing the coat.

But Chancho, of course somebody should have

watched him. He took his money and went out and wasted on the most unnecessary, useless, impractical thing he could find in the county. A tombstone for himself. But I suppose he enjoyed it. At least he was always inviting people to come see how nice he's gonna look when he's buried.

So that was the end of the story except one hot day, Dzea and I were sitting under the arbor in his new resort drinking a pitcher of chilled wine with fresh peaches cut in. Chancho was sleeping on the grass.

"This will be a better place for you, Dzea," I said, "than the lunch business—not so much hurry-up to it and especially no sandwiches."

"Yes," Dzea said, "I have to admit in my heart I was always ashamed of the sandwiches. Takes all the dignity out of eating, a sandwich. But you know it still wonders me how it ever happened your business picked up so quick. In all my years of experience I never heard of such a thing before."

Chancho woke up. "I drink wine now," he said. Dzea poured him glass.

"Puzzles me too," I said. "One day I was selling three hundred lunches, overnight it was a thousand, the next day three thousand. But why?"

"Was the money I put back in the business," Chancho said.

"Explain me, Chancho," Dzea said. "Simple way."

"I took the moneys I found in the flour bin," Chancho said, "and I changed into dollar bills. Yes. And I wrapped one in the bottom sangwiksh of every tenth box so people preferred to buy our lunch. I guess they was glad when they was finding. What you think?"

Toothpicks, health salt, tombstones, give dollar bills away—he was really without brains. Poor Chancho.

XI

THE BEING OF A SOLDIER

ONE day while I was still in Calistoga I happened
into the kitchen for something and there was Chancho running through the manual of arms with loaf of
French Bread for gun while Uncle John sat in his
chair and watched with a cloudy face.

"Bijo," Dzea said to me, "Chancho says you joined
the army so you could sell more lunches. That's a
serious thing."

"Not the real army," I said. "Only something like
it. The National Guard. But I didn't join to sell
lunches. In fact, just the opposite happened. I was
selling them about three hundred sandwiches and
three hundred milks every Sunday. Extra money
helped out O.K. But then I enlisted. 'Course if I'm
a soldier of the United States wearing her uniform,
carrying her gun, how can I sell sandwiches to my
country for a profit?"

"If you went of your own free will," Dzea said,
"then of course, it's impossible. Like making a profit
on your parents."

"Yes. So I gave for cost."

"But why you joined? Wasn't six years of hell in czar's army enough for you? Kicks and curses, wormy bread and sour stew?"

"I guess I'm like old cavalry horse when he hears the band," I said. "I was taking lunches every Sunday out to their rifle range and about the fourth week when I drove up—My God—what they're doing? Using my milk bottles for targets."

" 'Listen, boys, listen,' I said. 'Cost me cash, three cents each, those bottles—you'll bankrupture me.'

" 'Gee,' the lieutenant said, he was nice young man, twenty-three or four years old, 'I'm sorry, lunchman. We never gave it a thought. Look, fellows,' he called them all together. 'I'll pass around the hat; we fill it full of money; shoot again. One that wins gets the kitty; settles up with lunchman and keeps the rest himself. All right, lunchman?' "

" 'All right for me,' I said.

"So they collected $27.50 and now they were shooting.

" 'Lieutenant,' I said, when everybody finished. 'It's my milk bottles anyway, so how about giving me a turn to shoot, too?'

" 'Yes, yes,' everybody hollers, 'lunchman gonna shoot. Give lunchman a revolver. Lunchman gonna try, too.'

"They set up the bottles. I took the necks off the first fourteen. Fifteenth, I busted whole bottle."

"Nothing special," Dzea said, "considering you was sniper in the last war. I guess the worst man in your company could do that good or else he be back digging trenches again."

"True," I said, "but anyway they can't believe it. Lunchman has to do it again. So I gave little more distance and showed a coupla other tricks. Anyway I won the kitty."

"No wonder," Dzea said. "Is easy that kind of shooting. At milk bottles that can't shoot back."

"Anyway the finish of it was they enlisted me in the National Guard."

"Yes, yes," Chancho said, "And Giorgi Ivanitch let me come with him to the armory and watch him drill. Hup. Hup. I clapped every time he went by. Hup. Hup."

"What you do besides drill and listen to officers curse you?" Dzea said.

"Don't curse us," I told him. "Probably get court-martialed if they did. Besides I don't think it ever came in their heads. They nice young fellows— mostly was in college. You never saw officers like these. We go in the gym with them; eat supper to-gether in the restaurant. They sit in streetcars with us. Why once after I was sworn in I was again on target range and one sergeant was mad I beat his score so when lieutenant came by he complained I don't hold my feets in right position. Now here's where hell starts, I thought. But lieutenant only asked to see my score card. He looked at it. 'Got highest score here,' he said. 'Of course we got to have rules about how to hold your feet and lotsa other things, but don't forget rules is just to take up slack when the brains runs out.' "

"What else you do there?" Dzea said.

"We take courses."

"Courses?"

"Studies. Learn anything. Blacksmithing. Radio insides. Signaling. Automobiles. Anything. All free. Government pays."

"I never hears such a thing in my life," Dzea said. "Teaching soldiers. Letting them think. Soldiers supposed to be ignorant, way I always heard. Why they have this army anyway?"

"In America is National Guard because once enemies came and was grabbing everything for taxes and living in people's houses and eating their food away from them and people don't like."

"Naturally," Dzea said. "I don't like neither."

"So Americans decided they gonna fight these enemies and make them go home."

"Just right," Dzea said. "They done just right."

"But these enemies had a big army, good trained, thousands and thousands of them marching in ranks and Americans didn't have nothing but their guns and their guts. Just the same they went out to meet them and they fired from behind walls and back of trees and then they ran and loaded and fired again."

"Bang. Bang." Chancho said, aiming his bread. "BANG!"

"Ten men, fifty men, a hundred, five hundred. Pretty soon they had an army and they drived the enemy home."

"Good," Dzea said. "I be pleased to shake their hand. Was long time ago?"

"Hundred years or longer. So after Americans said we gonna have a militia, how they call, in every state so things be ready if people have to defend themselves again."

"Sounds quite interesting," Dzea said. "I suppose I be too old to join myself in?"

"I could ask lieutenant when I go back."

"Try," Dzea said. "Tell I have lots of experiences. I was in Crimeans War and against the Turks and mountain fighting—. Before I die I think I enjoy to march once in an army where you can be a soldier— and still be a man.

XII

FOR ALL BUT THE BREAKING
HEART

ONE of our boys, Illarion, worked in a big college. He had there duties to watch through a telescope at the stars and see they stayed all in their places and between times he taught the students what tricks he knew like the way to measure the sun and what gonna be the shortest distance to get up on the moon or where the comets hurrying when they go so fast by. He was, how they call in English, an astronomer.

It didn't pay much, his job, considering there was such lot a night shift to it, but Illarion, thank God, hasn't got the kind of heart that's always aching after money. No, his pleasure was study and more study, and now and then for recreation maybe to catch a couple of stars that weren't around before and give them nice names and write them down in book. That, and a glass of wine once a week with his friends, he'd be a perfectly satisfied man, Illarion.

Now it was his usual custom to meet us every Friday night in a restaurant and have a good time together with us. Because even if Illarion was big professor and sat on platforms with a black board to cover his head, and people bowing down, still when he came in a party he had sense enough to leave his education home and sing and dance and drink and tell stories and enjoy himself like a human being.

Well, came this Friday and he didn't show up. Boiled *beche* we ordered, too. That's a piece of veal shoulder boiled with herbs. His favorite.

"I hope nothing be wrong," Vactangi told us, "but Illarion reads too much. Specially out of those thick heavy books. I warned him it gonna give him trouble some day. Not even pictures in them to break up the pages."

"I don't believe it hurts him," Challico said. "Us Khevsouris has eyes like a eagle's. Ever I told you about my uncle? He could shoot——"

Yes, yes, but we not interested to hear all over again how Challico's uncle can hit a wild boar exactly through the center of the heart at half a mile. Makes at least a hundred tellings now and each time Challico's uncle gets farther and farther away from pig.

"Boar again?" Vactangi asked. "Watch out, Challico, pretty soon gonna have to kill him by radio, your uncle."

"Well maybe Illarion's busy," I said, to stop the argument. "Moon eclipsing or something, keeps him on the job."

So we didn't bother too much and it went until the next Friday. Still no Illarion.

"After all," Vactangi said, "now is something wrong. The moon can't be on a rampage every week. Have to go in a college, one of us, and find out what's the trouble."

So we appointed Challico for a committee. "O.K.," he said. "If my countryman is in danger I go after him. If it's my duty to rescue my friend, it don't matter what kind of a place you send me in. I gonna go."

Comes he back the next day with news we didn't like to hear. Illarion was sick, very sick.

"What's the matter with him?" Vactangi wanted to know. "Describe me how he's a sick."

"Well, he's in a place like a hospital that belongs to the college. They say nothing's wrong. They say only he's tired. But I think they're trying to fool us."

"Did you see him?"

"Yes, they took me in a room, Illarion is lying with his face to the wall. 'My God, man,' I told in Georgian, 'what's the matter?!' Nurse makes me, 'Ssssh. Don't excite your friend. He's just a little bit overworked. He finished up important research and now he's resting.' 'Resting!' I said. 'Must be he's sick.' 'No, he's not sick.' She has a smile, that lady, flashes off and on her mouth like a light bulb. Makes me nervous. 'Gotta be sick,' I insist, 'a grown man laying in bed in the middle of the daytime. Illarion!

What's the matter?' 'Nothing,' he says. He sounds weaker than an orphan lamb."

"Illarion? In a bed"? I said. "A hundred and ninety pounds? Six foot three-inch man?"

"So I went and asked the doctor, a big, big professor. He tells me Illarion was working too hard, and now they don't want him to get nervous broke down."

"Nervous broke down?" Vactangi asked. "What means that?"

"It's American sickness," I said. "When your brain ain't interested in you any more."

"Must be awful thing that. Except once in while I forget where I put something, otherwise I'm on good terms with my own brains. I can't imagine not getting along together O.K."

"Why can't he have his head cracked in from fight, or a dagger wound?" I said. "A bullet through his leg? Something, at least, that a person can understand. Nervous broke down!"

So we decided the best thing is to go all together in the hospital see what can we do.

He was in a bathrobe this time, sitting in chair, but no life at all to his face. "Illarion," I said, "man, you want to eat?"

"We had a lovely dish of spinach for lunch," starched lady taking care of him said, "and if we good—" She shook her finger at him, "we gonna eat nice cup custard for our supper. Aren't we?"

"Illarion," Vactangi said in Georgian, "want lamb? Stick of *shashlik*, good broiled? Give you blood."

Illarion shaked his head, no.

"A glass of good black wine," Challico proposed. "That brings your strength back."

"Maybe you like us to give you a little song to cheer you up." My suggestion.

"No, gentlemen. Not today." The starched lady was putting us out. "But you can come again tomorrow."

"Look, boys. We gotta do something quick," I said. We was walking home. "Dzea Vanno's coming back from Fresno tomorrow. Dzea's lived through eighty years now. Surely he must know the answer to a thing like this."

So immediately Dzea came home we told him the story. He thought it over while he smoothed a nice point to his beard. "Is he disappointed in love, Illarion?" he asked finally.

"No," Challico said, "can't be that. First time I was there, just to see if I can shake him up, I said, 'Illarion, a young lady stopped me downstairs and asked how is Mr. Illarion, today? As beautiful as running deer she was. Maybe you special friend?' He don't even turn his head."

"Well, only one solution then," Dzea Vanno said. "We'll have to try garlic sauce. I don't like man that boasts but it could make cripples to dance or mutes to sing; it would bring the dead alive, my garlic sauce. Can cure everything in fact but man in love."

"I agree a hundred per cent," I told. "I tasted already. Will open Illarion's appetite and if he eats naturally he has to get better."

"And if it doesn't help?"

"Then nothing be any use," Dzea said. "We might as well make plans where we gonna have his funeral party. He ought to be ashamed of himself, a young fellow, strong body, all his arms and legs on, to get sick. I'm a eighty-five years old. You ever see me lay in a bed to worry my friends?"

"There'll be plenty of time later to give him hell," Vactangi said. "Just now, let's we be practical. How we gonna give him this garlic sauce? If we try to take it in the hospital they'll smell us coming from the streetcar stop."

"I gonna phone," Challico said, "ask the doctor can we come and take our friend Illarion for a little ride?"

"Yes?"

"Then we drive some place, make a party, have the sauce."

"After one whiff such delicious aroma," I said, "can't refuse Illarion to take a bite of meat, a swallow of wine, and first thing we know he be all well again, our Illarion."

"But what thinks the hospital when he don't come back right away?"

"After we get him out we phone again and tell he likes to stay for a few hours more with us. We take good care of him."

"Where shall we go? In the park?"

"No. We can't build big enough fire there."

"Beach?"

"Much better. We go far down away from the towns."

"Full with bootleggers all those little beaches," Vactangi said. "They unload their boats there."

"That's just a story," Challico told him. "For my part, I hope we see some. I'm gonna get five, six gallons. Buy wholesale, that's the way to save money."

So we phoned; doctor said O.K. and we called for Illarion in our car.

"We gonna take you on the beach," we told him. "Make a nice party, all be in honor of you."

"I don't care."

"And build a fire. Make *shashlik*."

"I don't care."

"*Ajepsandal* Dzea seasoned special your taste?"

"I don't care."

He was like a clock with no tick to it.

We drove along the coast twenty, twenty-five miles to a nice quiet spot. Parked in a field and climbed down the path to the beach. Clean white sand, cliffs on three sides to break the wind. Ideal. We fixed a place for Illarion with blankets against a big log so he could face the ocean.

"Now cheer up," Vactangi told him. "Breathe the sea air. You'll be well in no time. Breathe deep."

Meanwhile Challico and me gathered driftwood

for the fire and Dzea Vanno began to make the sauce. In his wooden mortar he put the garlic pearls and salt and pepper and our herb kinsey, and a pinch of dill. Then with his pestle Pound—Pound—Pound—and between each pound, he added little drops of tarragon vinegar, and again Pound—Pound—Pound. When the whole thing turned smooth as cream and the aroma filled the air it was ready to eat.

Illarion, an invalid, couldn't eat *shashlik* off a stick so Vactangi arranged a few of the tenderest pieces of meat on a nice leaf for him, put a drop of sauce beside it, broke him bread.

Then we ate, drank our wine. The sauce made us so hungry we broiled a few more sticks of lamb again; had another little glass of wine. Uncle John told some stories. Vactangi played us tune on his *chongouri*.

And the whole time out of our eye corners we were watching Illarion. He ate, yes, but from his interest he might as well be chewing sawdusts.

"Well, there's no use to expect miracles," Challico said when him and me went down the beach for more driftwood. "Maybe he needs to eat twice even garlic sauce before it cures him. A severe case like this."

When we came back Challico tried to brighten up Illarion by remembering things about home. Both they were Khevsouris, these two, from villages way, way up in our mountains. Kind of odd peoples, these Khevsouris, in their habits. Still to this very day they're wearing the helmets and chain-mail coats left

over from the Crusades and jousting with lances and
if they don't have any real fights on a hand, for pas-
time they stage mock ones with each other. Bravest
fellows in the world, but not a lot of progress to them.

Usually Illarion liked to talk about this. He was
proud he was a Khevsouri and had a right to bring
his men through any gate of the Holy City wearing
arms and with all their battle flags flying. Only of
course I don't think he ever did it so far. And him
and Challico always enjoyed to show how they can
play with broadswords so big that most men couldn't
even lift them.

"Come on, man," Challico encouraged, "this is a
lonesome place. It won't bother nobody if we sound
some of the battle calls. The one from the siege before Acre? How about that?"

"No." Illarion didn't want.

"How about our rally that saved the day at Dory-
leum? We don't often get a chance like this. Holler
all we want."

"No."

"Allright, then I gonna sing and you keep me
chorus. Come on. 'The Frankish men they have a
Queen, Eléanor, Eléanor.' "

"No." Nothing suited.

So Vactangi tuned the strings on his *chongouri*
again, and we made a nice quartette, me and Uncle
John and Challico, and for fourth we had the waves

rolling in—Boom—Boom—Boom to carry our bass. Boom. Boom.

And, just in that minute when we were so happy with a glass in hand watching our fire burn gold and green and blue, a bullet spit the sand not ten feet back of us.

"Down," Dzea said and we went flat behind the log. The gun spattered again.

"Only BB's," Vactangi listened to the third burst, "and from one gun, air rifle."

"Still, I don't want in my skin," Challico told. "Why they shooting on us?"

"Why? That's your bootleggers you gonna buy wholesale from. Better forget it. Try instead to remember some undertaker that'll give you a funeral for half price."

The bootleggers were back of us. We could hear them talking.

"Must they come up while we sang," Dzea Vanno said. "Probably they expecting boats tonight. That's why they give us a hint to go away."

"Then why don't they tell us nice way?" Challico said. "How can we go now? Impossible! Means we runned away."

We stayed quiet for a few minutes behind the log. Dzea was on one side of me, Illarion at the end.

"How we gonna manage?" Challico whispered. "Maybe they rush us?"

Something moved on the beach. Was it a man?

No. I looked again. Maybe seaweed? Couldn't be sure. I nudged Dzea. He couldn't see nothing. Only a shadow.

"How we manage?" Vactangi was answering, "why we gonna manage usual way. Stick together and fight and when last man is left alone he can do how he pleases."

"Let's wait," Dzea said, "few ——"

Then we heard a bellow, a sound that split open the night like a cleaver.

"Son of gun!" Challico said, "it's Illarion."

I felt the place next to me. Empty! It was Illarion all right and he's still yelling. Would turn a person's blood to sherbet that noise he makes.

"I got the one with the gun," he was hollering. "Give me hand, boys, is two others left." He was on the ledge halfway down the path with them. And how he got there? Why naturally it was nothing for him to creep the length of the beach, walk straight up the cliff and then jump down on the bootleggers. Regular mountain goats, anyway, all these Khev-souris.

So we went up, too, and after a little damages all around, finally we got the whole bunch together and tied them up with our belts.

"Now we have an armistice," Dzea, our oldest man, was spokesman—"Why you shoot us?"

"You breaka law," fellows told him. Must be he was Italian. Not speaking so good English.

"I break the law," Challico said. "You're funny, huh? Maybe President don't allow no more picnics on beach? Is that it?"

"Yuh, we know your picnics," biggest Italian said and won't talk more.

"If you was nice fellows we'd let you go." Dzea said. "But how we know what you'll do? You're too wild."

"No." Illarion said. "No, we can't fool around. We have to go to the nearest farm, phone the police."

"Police?" big fellow hollered, "whassa matter you? Crazy? Bootleggers."

"I don't care if you are or not," Illarion said, "but you can't shoot people. Dangerous. It's your own fault we have to call the police."

"You won't call the police," second fellow, red handkerchief on a neck, was speaking. The third bootlegger so far only made mumble, mumble. I don't know what was wrong with him. "You don't fool us. Police look two years for you. They lock you up in two minutes, you bootleggers!"

"We bootleggers?" Vactangi said. "You the bootleggers."

"You! You!" Big Italian was so mad he's jumping. "You! You!"

"Wait," Dzea Vanno said. "Let's get it straight who's who. I'm a man, by trade a cook, living in San Francisco. I comed here on a picnic. These my friends all. So you're the bootleggers, isn't it?"

"Certainly not," Big fellow talked. "I'm a farmer. This my two neighbors. Week after week all the gangsters unloading their boats here ——"

"Yes," Red Handkerchief put in his word, "and tramp down our artichoke fields carrying stuff to the trucks. Ruin my crops. I told to stay away ten times. No stay. So tonight I and my friends wait for when they get drunk like usual sing, holler, then we fill fulla pepper shot."

"Well," Challico said politely, "mistakes can happen, isn't it true?"

I untied the belts.

"How about damages?" Big Fellow wanted to know. "All our clothes tore. And your friend bent my rifle over his knee."

"Hocked hall my heeth hout," the little fellow, the mumbling one, crept around on the ground lighting matches. "Han't hind. Hup. No, hat's a hock. Houldn't I hollowed, hould I?"

"His teeth are gone," Red Handkerchief told us.

"My God," Illarion said, "I didn't mean to do that."

"False teeth," Red Handkerchief explained. "Could be worse."

"Well, we very, very sorry, anyway," Dzea Vanno said. "Would fifteen dollars make our apology?"

They guessed it would.

"O.K. boys," Dzea told us, "get together money."

"No, I gonna pay," Illarion said. "I feel good. I didn't feel so good in years. Let it be my treat."

So we paid over the money. Shook hands all around. "Now we friends." Dzea Vanno said.

"Pardon me," Little One said, he found his teeth and got them in, "ain't you eating something with garlic in?"

Well next thing they were down on the beach and we broiled more lamb and Big Fellow, Tony was his name, sent Red Handkerchief home across the fields for two jugs. "I gonna give you drink good wine," he promised.

And Illarion, my God, he was eating and singing and doing somersaults backwards, and showing us how they dance in his village and shaking himself all over like happy dog got off a chain.

Finally fire was out; food all gone; songs all sung, our party was over. "Son a gun!" Tony said, after they promised to come the next Sunday and visit us in the city, "I never see fellows fight so good. You must like, huh? Zim-Zam," he smacked his fists in his hand. "Must be a regular hobby for you boys?"

It was after eight o'clock in the morning when we deposited Illarion back in college. "Don't take me to the hospital," he told us. "Leave me off at my room." He felt full of snort and ready to get on his job.

"Well, Dzea," Challico said when we were driving down our street, "just like you promised. That garlic sauce, it cures everything."

"Everything," Dzea said twinkling his eyes. "Everything but a man in love."

"And what cures that, Dzea?" I asked him.

Dzea smoothed the white wings of his mustache. "Only the grave," he said, "or another prettier face."

XIII

TO BE HAPPY MARRIED

NATURALLY when I engaged myself for marriage with Helena Gerbertovna I went right away with heartful of happiness to carry the good news to my friends.

But seemed like they weren't so pleased. Vactangi showed long horse face. Challico sat dark blue in a corner. Even Illarion, practically American himself now, didn't give me any support. Only Dzea shaked my hand and that sadly. "You take a big chance, Bijo, to marry with an American girl." All he said.

"First place," Vactangi pointed out, "American young ladies don't like foreigner names. Now you have to change yours. One Russian, I knew him well, immediately he married American young lady she made him go in court take the name of Gerbert Goover. For honor. Next election Gerbert Goover don't wins. How he feels then, that Russian fellow? Be same with you."

"Main thing," Illarion said, "the American girls I met so far can only cook out of books."

"See. Something else you didn't know," Vactangi said. "Lose the book. Ph-i-i-i-t-t. No eat. You'll starve."

"I can buy another book," I said.

"And what's more" Challico had his turn, "Americans cooking every day just enough. Two peoples, two steaks. Three peoples, three steaks. Never cook' ing one extra piece for the pot's good luck. Company comes unexpected they gonna sit hungry. You'll die from shame before you're six months married."

"Yes," Vactangi said, "and after your funeral there won't be any table either. Maybe a cup a tea for who carries your burial box. I won't come."

"Never enjoy the pleasure at mealtime to call in strangers passing on the road to share your table." Challico shook his head. "Won't even be any use to get rich. You'll have a shiny white five-hundred dollar, pull-a-button, push-a-button refrigerator and not one extra piece of baloney to keep inside."

"But you don't know the worst thing that's gonna happen in your house," Vactangi warned. "American young ladies all keep bodguts."

"Helena Gerbertovna has dog," I said. "Irishman setter named Veleike Kneeaz. Comes 'Duke' in English. But that's all."

"Bodguts means writing down moneys before you spending," Vactangi explained. "Suppose you not feeling good, we take for example. You want to stop in Russian Club drink glass of vodka, eat piece herring maybe, for your stomach. You have to write down in bodguts first:

I'm drinking whiskys..........35c
Eating piece herring, too........10c

"Where you ever knew American young lady to find out such informations?" I asked him.

"That's enough, boys," Dzea said. "If they promised to each other can't help now. Damage is done." He shook my hand again. "Never mind, I stood your friend twenty years, Bijo Gogio, and I don't stop now."

Well, I didn't pay attentions to them and everything was fine. First time in my life I had a family— best mother a man could want, a sister with a sweet face that smiled, even a grandmother. Should have everybody a grandmother to make a dignified ornament for the house.

So I lived under a bright blue sky in my shining world until the day came the ladies was planning for the wedding company.

"If you want to invite ten or eleven people," My Mother said to me, "and fifteen more here—we'd better count on about thirty, I suppose. Patty shells, three, no, four chickens, mushrooms ——"

Four chickens. This was a terrible situation. But better I tell now what kind of countrymen I have than they find it out at the table. "Dzea Vanno can eat two chickens alone by himself," I said, "when he's in good appetite."

My Mother looked surprised. "Goodness, doesn't it give him high blood pressure?"

"Seems healthy enough," I said, "for man eighty-five anyway."

"Well, more chickens then and French peas, those *petits pois*, and tiny hot biscuits. Then a mousse ——"

"Moose be O.K.," I said, "can make *shashlik* from haunches and boil up the shoulders—" I saw Helena Gerbertovna was laughing.

"Mousse is like ice cream," Sister whispered to me.

Just showed you never can tell. For me is like elk. But I didn't say anything.

"Look, dear," My Mother suggested. "Suppose we do it this way. You tell us about a wedding breakfast in Georgia and then we'll see what we can manage."

"They never stop at breakfast," I said. "They eat all day."

"Well, what do they have?"

"First is fishes," I said, "maybe white sturgeon smoked over hickory and mountain trout fried crispy in sweet butter and *zootki*, that's like bass, with a sauce of carrot and dill and bay and then *satules* and sprats and *oragueli*, a *kalmaki*, he's a big fish baked with a slice of lemon in his mouth. Then little caviar for anybody likes it dusted over with chopped chives and let's see ——"

"Sounds like real good shore dinner back to hum

in the state of Maine," The Grandmother said. "You folks ever eat lobster?"

"Not usually," I told her, "but wouldn't do any harm to put three or four on the table. Maybe somebody likes to try them. I guess that be enough for the fish."

"What comes next?" Sister asked. She was writing it all down with pencil."

"*Satskali Katzis-Kzilala* means 'poor man's caviar,' " I said. "We always have that. It's easy. Scoop whole baked eggplants out of their skins and mash up with fine, fine chopped green baby onions, lemon juice, oil, tarragon, and parsleys."

"Oil, tarragon, eggplant," My Mother was repeating faintly, "sturgeon, caviar——"

"The soup we can skip," I said, "so next comes meats. First the roast turkeys with *t'sat t'sivi* sauce. Is Dzea Vanno's speciality, *t'sat t'sivi* sauce and—wait—" That gave me idea. "With your kind permission how would it be if I asked Uncle John to come few days early and he can manage everything?"

"You mean he's a cook?" My Mother said.

"He had restaurant for years and years," I said. "Don't worry more."

"Well," My Mother breathed a big sigh, "that will be just fine. He'll tell us what to order and Helen can watch him and learn some dishes for you. It doesn't make any difference how much he charges. A caterer. We should have thought of that before."

What means caterer? Should I ask? No. If it's about food Dzea will manage it.

So I made the arrangements and few days before the wedding I went to the station to take Dzea Vanno off the train. He's so surrounded with packages and cartons and suitcases I told him he looks like mother hen with chicks.

"Well, I couldn't decide which my *cherkasskas* to bring, boy," he said. "My black one with the sable hat or my white one with the astrakhan. So I finally made a choice and bringed both. Then there's my soup kettle and some herbs probably can't get in place like this and—" Named over a dozen articles he can't live without.

I picked everything up and stowed in car. Everything, that is, except the velvet portfolio where Uncle John carried his big desperate butcher knives, the wicked-bladed slicers, his curved-edged corers, the choppers, and little fancy cutters, sharp as a razor. This nobody was ever allowed to touch except Dzea himself. Artist's tools.

We drove home and I took him in hall.

"Is that the man to cook?" My Mother said.

Dzea was sorting his luggages and taking out this and that, but soon he heard lady's voice he looked in mirror gave last pull to his coat and made an entrance. First he bowed to room, then he kissed hands all around, next he presented bouquet of red roses to The Grandmother, offered satin box of fruit glacé to My

Mother, gave Sister a bottle of perfume tied with bow, and made a speech in Georgian. When he finished that he found small jeweler's box in his pocket for Helena Gerbertovna, kissed me on both cheeks and sat down.

The Grandmother got her breath back first. "Much obliged. But what did he say?"

"He thanks you for the honor of your invitation," I said, "and he wishes a long life in a happy family together for us all. He regrets I don't have no mother, and my father is so far away but he will be pleased to act my nearest relative in all ceremonies necessary."

"Thank him for us, please," My Mother said. "Express our appreciation."

Uncle John spoke again.

"He says," I explained, "that to save the ladies the trouble of writing long lists for the party he gives himself the pleasure of accompanying you to the market tomorrow. He helps you choose everything."

"Can't we talk with him?" Sister asked.

Uncle John had himself pretty well collected together by this time and he understood the question. He rose. "I luff you," he said in English. "I luff you all," and sat down again.

So for next few days the house was full of party, and from early morning you couldn't hear anything but the sound of chopping, stirring, rolling, pound-ing, oven doors snapping open and shut, tops of pots dancing with steam. And Dzea was having grand time—peeking in bins and counting silverwares and popping in and out of pantry to look over each new dishes came down off the shelf and twirling empty wineglass in his fingers while he thinked up next new dish he could surprise us with.

First day Dzea and The Grandmother had some sharp words over what makes right brine for pickled peppers, but like many quarrels they was the better friends afterward, especially when it came out they was both great believers in the principle of the bean, baked, boiled, fried, in soup, and in salad, as man's best friend.

Then there was ladies that came to call and Uncle John was always having long tête-à-têtes with them about best way to candy quinces or hearing confidential details about a certain angel cake recipe they knew. For his spare minutes house was full of cooking gadgets he never tried before—slicer for making dried apples, carved butter mold, and if you can imagine it he even proposed I take apart some kind of special coffee grinder, almost heirloom, came around the Horn with Helena Gerbertovna's great-grandfather, just so he can see how it pulverizes coffee so fine.

Naturally I had no time for foolishness like this. I needed my whole days to memorize the wedding service so I don't disgrace my friends and my country in the critical moment.

At last the great day came; the ceremony was over and I'm a married man. And after all the congratulations were said and we got enough good wishes to furnish our life for a century it came time to sit down at the beautiful table where candles shone and roses bloomed and the food—well maybe some of the American guests were little surprised and shocked to see this different kind of wedding refreshment. But not so surprised they couldn't eat with brisk appetite and not so shocked they didn't come back for second, and might as well tell the truth, third and fourth helpings.

As for my friends, when they saw table Challico was man enough to make me apology and even Vactangi admitted he didn't see any better since his uncle's daughter got married. So everybody was happy.

Meantime Uncle John was sitting in midst of American ladies humming like a buzzlebee in a bouquet of flowers and darting his head this way and that. "So we pound nuts to paste," I heard him say, "then we mix with chopped onions——"

"Raw onion?" Ladies was leaning forward with all attention.

"Yes, madame, but don't be alarmed. We cut his claws, because next comes lemon juices and then a pepper ——"

"Sweet pepper?"

"Sweet as lady's smile," Uncle John bowed. "Sweet

green bell pepper. Then parsleys and kinsey, our special herb, and we mash it all with fresh young green beans ———"

"Delightful," lady with piled up curls sang, "perfectly delightful."

"And that's our *m'tswane lobeo*."

So time passed. There were some toasts and some tears and lots of laughing and at last came hour we had to leave because we were going on a trip. Then, of course, everybody remembered one last thing they forgot to say before and Helena Gerbertovna had another costume to put on and after that she must cut few more slices of wedding cake and throw her bouquet. And the tickets? Where's my train tickets?

"Where you put the train tickets? Illarion. Quick!"

He said, "In your wallet."

What kind of place was that to hide train tickets? But Thank God, I found.

And now just before we were ready to leave Uncle John made an excuse to find Helena Gerbertovna in the hall and he told her a long secret. It was so important he must have repeated it over twice, because through the archway I could see her nod yes. And again, yes.

But at last we were on our way. Person can enjoy to have one wedding but for my part I don't think I could ever live through two.

"So now," I said to Helena Gerbertovna, we were in the train, "Let's don't start our home by keeping secrets from each other. What Uncle John told you?"

She's laughing. "Another recipe."

"My God," I said, "what was this one for?"

" 'If you want to be happy married,' he whispered in my ear, 'at least once a day say to your husband, 'I love you!' And whenever you set a table for Georgians, remember—only too much is ever enough.' "

XIV

I LAUGH—BUT NOT OUT LOUD

EVEN with best advices in the world still it's hard for an American girl to marry with a foreigner and learn different ways, different food, different language.

But I must say, everything considered, my wife, Helena Gerbertovna, got along pretty well. She learned how to make *ajepsandal*, that's onions fried until they turn to golden rings, then mixed with baked eggplant and tomatoes, and she got to be very good at corn bread. She even picked up a few words in Georgian and she made the acquaintance of my countrymen. Only mostly, with the exception of Dzea Vanno, they were all so long from home they acted more like Americans.

In fact only once Helena Gerbertovna ever got off on her wrong feets and still when I remember it makes me laugh—but not out loud if Helena Gerbertovna can see me.

A short time before I married I had good luck with an invention I made. All my life I was making inventions just for fun. When I was about ten years old I invented a wooden gun with wooden bullets and I shot a rabbit with it. And the only thing about the war I enjoyed was the piles of junk machinery we had, all so badly made that whatever you did to them was an improvement.

Now I found out that in America they're crazy about any kind of inventions, especially those that work, and they're glad to pay good money for them. The trick is to find a way to make simple something that's hard to do or else figure out a complicated process for easy things so they look more important.

A short time after we married I was working with duplicating paper. Nothing very interesting but to be near the place it was made we moved to the South, a small town in Virginia. No Greeks or Syrians or Russians in that town. Nobody. I guess I was the only foreigner inside the city limits.

After we were there a few weeks we had a letter from Eliko in New York.

Is one our countryman, Besso Pecswelashvily, in North Carolina [he wrote]. Living there for years and years. From long time back. Only nobody knows where. He's lost from us. Now he's your neighbor it be your duty to find him.

So I told Helena Gerbertovna some day when we have spare time we'll go and find Besso Pecswelashvily. Only I was busy finishing up with the paper and

besides, I had my head full of a new kind of waterproof cement I wanted to try out.

Then one day I smelled spring in the air. Especially
beautiful springs they have there in Virginia and in
a week the meadows were running blue with grape
hyacinths and under the trees violets with leopard
leaves made golden carpets and everywhere, everywhere was perfume from the pine trees.

"Time to have an adventure," I said to Helena
Gerbertovna. "How about we try to find Besso?"

So we locked the house, took the dogs and started
off in the car. I had a general idea from Eliko's
letters where this Besso lived. It was supposed to be
a small town east of Durham that began with C or K
and there wasn't no railroad station and a river ran
near by.

Helena Gerbertovna made me a list out of the
almanac of places that might do. "But how will we
manage?" she said. "You can't go door to door and
ask."

"I'll find main restaurant," I said, "and ask the
proprietor. If the man is a Georgian and in the town,
sometimes he was having party there if only for himself."

First two days no luck. We used up almost all our
towns. Third evening we heard of one old man that
might fit. But it turned out he was an Armenian,
sixty years from Kars. We stayed a coupla hours in
his house and heard his life story and looked at his

photographs and met his family and drank up a bottle of *duzika* with him. *Duzika* is a drink that tastes like licorice candy only it's whisky and for my part it isn't any more agreeable than it sounds.

So I asked this Armenian if ever he met a man, Besso Pecswelashvily. He says no but they say some foreigner lives in the next town forty-six miles away. Whether by foreigner they mean a foreigner from Pennsylvania, from Russia, or even from the moon he doesn't know. All foreigners to these people. So far he didn't visit him.

We decided to try it and we drove over. It was almost evening when we got there. And for Eliko's information, the town didn't begin with *C* or *K*; it wasn't east of Durham and there was only half a river, the rest dried up in summer.

A colored was walking on the road and I stopped and asked him about the man I was looking for. Such rich voices they have, those coloreds, like honey pouring out from a silver pitcher.

"Yes," he told us, "some kind of a man, not an American, lives in the last house on the main road. Turn right. Then left."

We found it. A dark house. No light. I pounded and pounded. Nobody came. I went back in car.

"Nobody home?" Helena Gerbertovna said.

"No. I leave a note and if it's him maybe some-time he comes to see us."

"And if it isn't maybe he comes anyway," Helena Gerbertovna said. "It wouldn't surprise me."

I wrote a few words, stuck them under the crack, gave the door one more bang for good luck and started away. That minute a panel in the door opened and face looked out at me. "*Gamarjueba*, May ever thou be victorious when thou art in battle," I said to the face.

Face went away. Panel closed, I'm waiting. Nothing happened. I'm waiting again. Still nothing.

"Listen," I said to the door in Georgian. "I think who lives behind you is crazy and his father was crazy and before that his grandfather. I hope, who-ever you are, that your next piece of bread turns to stone in your mouth and you don't find one friend to sit down at your table until the day of your funeral party. And if I be alive that time then I give myself the pleasure to visit your house again. Good night!" If he be Georgian, he understood my opinion of him. If not, no harm done.

Door opened. A man came out, maybe forty, fifty years old.

"*Gage Marjos*," he said. His voice cut off the words like a rusty saw. "May the victory go to you. Have to excuse me. Come into my house."

"My wife is in the car," I said.

"With your permission," he said, "I be pleased to ask her to come in, too."

So we went in and sat down. Kind of a shabby house inside, but clean.

"I take back about your father and grandfather," I said, "but I still think you're crazy. Why don't you let me in the first time?"

"I don't want to know nobody," he said. "I'm a miser. I want everybody to go away. Leave me alone."

"In that case why did you let me in at all?" I said.

"When I heard your voice I split in half. I don't know what to do. Turn away my countryman? Let you go and say ever after, 'I knocked at the door of Besso Pecswelashvily, but the door stayed closed against me'? I wouldn't have no face left. So I had to let you in."

"Well," I said, "I suppose the explanation is that you was a Georgian first before you took up being a miser. And like they say, 'To the first trade ever the hand returneth.' "

He was laying the table for us and he shaked his head, yes, but doesn't say anything more.

To keep the room from filling up with silence I said, "Quite interesting. You're the first man I ever met from any of us that don't like company. Usually it's our fault to be too much the other way."

"Well," he said, "if I'm acquainted with people they borrow from me. They have sick relatives and need money to cut them open; or start some sure business; or buy a piece of property. It's always the same. Inventions especially. That's my biggest weakness. Put money in people's inventions." He looked at me from under his eyebrows. "You don't have anything like that, do you?"

"No," I said. "I like to invent things but I don't need any money for them."

"Haven't got nothing buzzing in your head just now, have you? Some little idea? ——"

Why shall I tell him about my cement? I thought. I rather work it out myself. "One thing for an engine," I said, "but I'm not much interested. I think it's perpetual motion, anyway, but I need a locomotive to make sure."

"Had to be. Had to be," Besso beat his head. "Can't escape. I'm the worst for perpetual mobile than for anything. Well, explain me how it works, your idea. Maybe we can manage the locomotive."

To change the conversation I said, "My dogs are in the car. Is it all right if I bring them in?"

When I came back he had two big dishes of meat on the floor. Keddana and Murka helped themselves with good appetite.

"Maybe they're still hungry," he said watching them shine up the plates.

"No," I said, "they had plenty."

He put a package of cupcakes down before each one. Keddana had enough manners to scratch the wrappings off his before he ate, but Murka wasn't so much in society before and she swallowed the wax paper and all.

After this he made a nice table and we sat down and had a good time. He told me his life and I told him mine. He was especial pleased to find me only married so short a time that I paid him the honor to bring my wife in his house.

He went over to the wall and moved a picture away. Underneath it was a big hole in the wall, the plaster and laths all broken. He put his hand in and pulled out a set of opal earrings. I never saw such pretty things—they looked like a pair of soap bubbles set in gold. "I wish to give myself the pleasure of presenting your wife with this little souvenir. Do I have your permission?"

I said he could with my sincere appreciation. But Helena Gerbertovna made some excuse to refuse.

"Certainly, certainly," he said, "my stupidity. You will forgive me. You think opals are bad luck, isn't it?" He reached in the hole and brought out such a pin for a collar from amethyst. "I ask your permission," he said to me, "to offer this brooch instead. Or this." He showed a diamond ring.

Helena Gerbertovna took the pin with thanks before the presents got any more serious.

"You can't be no miser," I told him. "Impossible."

"Yes, yes," he said. "Must I am. Otherwise I wouldn't keep jewelry in the walls. Now would I?"

So finally came time for us to go home. He insisted I take for a present a pair of binoculars. "So you'll remember the first time you were in my house" and a camera "to remind you of your journeying days and nights through a strange land to find your country-man," and only when I told she had six or seven extra ones already Helena Gerbertovna got away without having to accept a typewriter that could spell in English, Russian, or Greek letters. He promised us he would come and return our visit in the third week after this.

Now on our ride back home Helena Gerbertovna was bubbling over with questions. Why was he so quiet? Why didn't he talk directly to her? Didn't he like her?

"He's from the old style," I said. "That's how they were acting years and years ago. They had cast-iron manners those days—no bend to them. It was supposed to be polite."

So we got home and I went back to work and finally I finished up my cement and I was pretty sure it was OK. I said to Helena Gerbertovna, "I'm going to cement the basement of this house." It was a dampy drippy place. "If it works there then I know I really invented waterproof cement." I made good job of it and the basement was dry as bone. We used to go down there five or ten times a day to look at it. My masterpiece!

So the day Besso was supposed to come I went to the train to meet him. But on my way I saw a red fox run under a bridge and I investigated him awhile, trying to find out why hippopotamuses, for example, are for sculpture, but foxes not and I came to conclusion, if there is any answer, it must be in their tails. Then I found a wild orchid, how they call a lady's shoe, and I dug that up for Helena Gerbertovna's garden. Then I wondered if I could catch any words out of what the brook was saying. I laid down on the ground and listened and listened. But it only seemed to bubble, "Fishes in dishes—fishes in dishes," and that reminded me I'm hungry so I got up went on to depot.

Train had already entered the station and passed out again. About half, three quarters of an hour ago agent tells me. No Besso. I decided he didn't come because surely he's not such an impractical man he expects me to be on time. If he comes he must have common sense enough to know I'm late and wait for me.

So I went home. There on the porch with the cold wind whipping around was Helena Gerbertovna with a sweater and a scarf and gloves pouring tea for Besso who's wearing a muffler, an overcoat and a hat with a kind of a horrified face under it.

Well, we moved inside and I tried to figure out what bothers Besso but whatever it was, it wore off pretty soon and he unpacks the presents he brought, a guitar for me and a pair of skis for Helena Gerbertovna. "All American girls like athletics," he said.

We finished lunch, drank, had a good time and then he had to go to Richmond on business, but he said he'll be back the following day on his way home. Helena Gerbertovna could hardly wait for him to make his farewell. The seams on her curiosity were almost ready to burst.

"What was the matter?" she said as soon as he was out the door, "For heaven's sake why wouldn't he come in the house with me?"

"What happened?" I said.

"Well, he knocked on the door and of course I shook hands and told him to come in. I'm sure I was pleasant. I was glad to see him. But he says he'll wait for you outside. I insist he comes in. But no he sits down in a porch chair so I went outside, too. I talked about every subject I could think of—the weather, Virginia, and the other Georgians I knew, his trip. I looked around, still you didn't come and it was after one o'clock and so I brought our lunch outside. What's the matter with him? Did I do something?"

"No, no, that's the manners from old, old times," I said. "Years and years ago it was the custom when you go first time to a man's house you're supposed to wait outside until he bids you in himself. Just a habit. Not supposed to be courteous anyway," I said, "to go into man's house when he's gone and his wife is there alone."

"Oh my heavens," Helen Gerbertovna almost choked all of a sudden and her face turned pink as roses. "What I did! What I did!"

"What?"

"After I took him around the garden and showed him the arbor you made and the fishpond, and ——"

"Well, what?" I said.

"I—what I did! I disgraced you forever." She started to cry. "I couldn't think of anything else to entertain him so I said, 'How would you like to go down the basement with me and I'll show you the cement?'"

XV

SO WE BOUGHT A FARM

Two things happened at once second spring we lived
in Virginia. Emilia Jacalevna, she was Elia's wife,
promised she gonna spend her summer vacation with
us and I tried to persuade Helena Gerbertovna to
enter a contest. Why you specially liked some kind of
oil for cooking, was problem involved.

"It's kind of oil you use anyway," I said. "Why
don't you try?"

"Don't be silly," Helena told me. "Real people
never win those contests. It's the company's aunt out
in Iowa that gets the prize or maybe just a made-up
person."

"I don't believe," I said. "So many people winning
things all the time in America, every page in the
newspaper; every hour on the radio. Surely they must
be real, those people. Looks like it's regular industry
in America, winning contests."

"Well, you try then."

So I wrote letter to oil company:

Greetings to who these words shall come. May all be well with you. I have pleasure to inform you my wife prepares every day salad with dressing from your oil. Whether it's my wife or your oil, I wouldn't say, but of this I'm sure—no better salad any man ever ate.

I won a furnace, a stoker and eight tons of coal.

Helena Gerbertovna was furious. She's supposed to be the literary composer for our family. So to pay me back she jumped over the fence into my world and invented a collapsible flower pot and way to make weather stripping out of old inner tubes and sold the ideas to a mechanical magazine. Good luck to anybody that tries to make either of them. And now we were even.

But meantime about the furnace. We lived in a rented house and besides there was no place to install another heater anyway so the salad oil company very kindly gave me an electric refrigerator instead.

"And now let's we be practical," I said, after it was installed and humming in the kitchen. "Better we buy a house and the next time we have a place all ready for the prize whatever it is. No use to keep making the same mistakes."

So we bought a farm in Pennsylvania.

But all this was second to Emilia Jacalevna's promise to give us her vacation, quite an unexpected honor. Because Emilia Jacalevna was a very busy fashionable lady with an enormous wardrobe, two fur coats and a different hair combing for every day in the week. And at this time she owned a glittery beauty shop and gave marcelling demonstrations before packed ballrooms at the Astor. And she was always telling us how to act and be and do "in real American style."

Well, we moved to the farm few days before Emilia's vacation began and after our furniture was all put in the wrong rooms and the broken things swept up and the telephone installed I said, "Now I guess I call Elia and give him the directions for Emilia Jacalevna's coming."

"Someway I can't imagine Emilia Jacalevna," Helena said, "with her dove's blood nail polish and fretwork stockings out on a farm. But go ahead."

I got the number. "Eliko," I spoke in Georgian. "We moved from Virginia yesterday. We moved here. Tell Emilia Jacalevna to come to us just the same. Tell her come on the train to Bethlehem. Same how we explained before. From Pennsylvania Station . . . only to Bethlehem . . . not to Richmond. You understand?"

"Yes," Eliko said, "Certainly." He was speaking so close to the mouthpiece that his voice dripped out into our room. "I understand."

"Pennsylvania Station?"

"Yes."

"Tuesday, like we said."

"Yes."

"All right. Good-by."

"Wait," Eliko shouted. "But where you want her to come?"

I got tight hold on the phone. "Beth-le-hem. In Pennsylvania."

"I no get it. Spell."

"Beh-eh," I began, but there is no *th* in Georgian. I made glutteral *h'ugh*.

"I'm not hearing," Eliko screamed. "Sounds like Beagle. Is such a town, Beagle?"

"How do I know?" I said. "Pay attention. Bethlehem. Beh-eh-h'—oh hell—where the steel is. Steel, man, steel."

"You want her to come to Pittsburgh, maybe?" Elia inquired. "You meeting in Pittsburgh station?"

"Look," I braced my feet. "Eliko, City of Bethlehem. Bethlehem where Christ was born."

"He was born in old country," Eliko said, "I know that. No place here."

I could feel my rage start to boil but I tried again. "Bethlehem. Like your *ochestvo*, your father's name. Got it? O.K. And tell Emilia Jacalevna to call us from the depot."

"Now I understand," Eliko said. "Why you not saying before? She be there. Good-by."

I hung up and wiped off my forehead. "I should have thought of that first. Now he's got it."

"But his father's name wasn't Bethlehemovich. He surely can't be called Elia Bethlehemovich?" Helena said.

"No. But just like it. Bartholomew. Elia Bartholomovich. She'll find it now."

We waited Tuesday and Wednesday and all of Thursday, but no Emilia Jacalevna. Friday afternoon the station agent called.

"There's a lady," he said, "that's been waiting here quite some time now and I have an idea she might belong to you folks."

We hurried to the station. It was Emilia Jacalevna looking as usual like a stranger in a new dress, a new hat, a new hair combing and a new make-up.

"So," she said, she was laughing like anything. "You no meeting me. I wass in Bechtelsville already, a nice place, and in Barto, I took postcards there, and I wass in New Jerusalem, too. I wass all over. I wass two days in here. Wass funny to see the peoples. They think you never come for me."

"We're terribly, terribly sorry," Helena said. "We're awfully sorry ——"

"Doesn't make difference," Emilia said, "because I know you will come. Sometime."

So we drove home and unloaded the wardrobe case and the leather make-up kit and the two hatboxes and the valise and the shoe carrier, but an Emilia Jacalevna we never knew before followed them out of the car.

"Iss farm," she said, arching her neck and breathing toward the barn. "Iss farm. Why you not telling? Come on——" She pulled off her spiky-heeled shoes and her stockings and started out barefoot across the yard.

She looked at barn with a sharp eye for the beams, investigated pigsty, shaked her head over the chicken houses, circled the oat field to pull several heads for chewing, lumped good handfuls of dirt in every field, walked the creek length and finally with us still trailing after, came home and sat down under the catalpa to think.

"Iss not good for chickens, this farm," she said at last. "Too damp. Iss not good for potatoes. Too sticky. Iss not good for barley, too, maybe. But iss a good farm. A fine farm. Now we make the arrangements. What to do? Wheat? Rye?"

"We thought we wouldn't plant anything," Helena Gerbertovna told her. Then she saw Emilia's face. "That is—hardly anything. Just some—oh—tomatoes and cucumbers and things. We thought mostly we'd live here like a house but not like a farm. The fields can stand."

"Then would be weeds," Emilia said. "Why, on half such a farm as this—on quarter such a farm—a man would be rich at home for his whole life, and send his children to school and wear a golden watch with a golden chain."

"Oh, I don't think there's much money in farming, Emilia Jacalevna," Helena said. "Farming isn't a thing that pays, although it must be lots of fun."

"Pay? Why on this farm in a stone house with

three, four, six—" she knocked them off on her fingers—"eight rooms and a spring cellar and pens and such kind of barn lives the richest farmer in the country. He has pigs and cows and horses in his fields, and his mows be full of hay, this farmer, and his bins full of grains. To speak with him at the market iss an honor. Have to plant. And first on a farm iss to plow."

"My father sold our own raised horse, Challa," I told her, "and with the money he sent me to Vladikavkaz to take a trade. At the droshke station he was not ashamed to weep, my father. He said to me, 'Go, my son, and learn and you will not have to walk after a plow all your life like me—to earn your bread in bitterness.' My father said that. Besides I don't like farming."

"If life gives, you have to take," Emilia said. "Can't help. Iss fate. In our village wass a man and drawing water he fell into the well. He screams and screams. The neighbors pulled him out with ropes and a hook. He said, 'Thank God.' But he said Thank God too soon, that man. In the war they took him for a sailor. On the 'Kronstadt' a wave washed him over. He drowned. Left a wife, father, mother, three children. The water wanted him. That's all. Can't help. Iss fate. How about pigs?"

"No pigs," I said, "only pigs I'm gonna have is wild boars, a few, just for our own eating."

"Cows, then? Barn full of smooth brown cows to

give cream. We scrub one room all clean to make
butter in. And sheep—few sheep for the pastures
shows nice. And chickens—red chickens. The red
ones iss looking richer than plain white."

"If I get wild boars," I said, "I'm gonna hang the
hams without smoke from the ceiling of the room
where a bright fire burns. And the fat will drop—
drop—drop—in pearls—drop—drop, and when the
ham I can see through it like through a window glass
we have a party and eat. Like nuts it tastes, ham from
wild boars."

"O.K. Pigs, then." Emilia said. "I have a secret
from my mother for pigs. A kind of mash warm at
noon with milk. Maybe with the pigs we winning the
prize from the government. Iss such things here,
isn't?"

"Oh I suppose so," Helena said. "From the Department of Agriculture or the county fair or something."

"And you know," Emilia went on, "to such a rich
farm as this in bad times the poors are coming and the
orphans and the crippled people, all with the little
baskets for help. And you giving. From such a rich
farm you can afford. They bless you, those peoples,
and you thank God, He's letting you be the one to
help His poors."

"Personally," Helena said, "if any such thing ever
happened to me I'd be so embarrassed I'd drop dead.
Besides they go to the community chest."

" 'What thou keepest is lost,' " I recited. " 'What

thou givest is forever thine.' Lines from our great poet
S'hota Rustaveli. But charity is no good. Have to
show people better ways."

"They asking you advices, too," Emilia said. "How
to live, how to marry, how to die. And you tell them
answers. All those books, those journals you reading,
Helena, that wouldn't be wasted now."

"Not knowing how to live myself," Helena said
crossly, "I certainly wouldn't tell anybody else how."

In silence we sat and listened to the doves, mourn-
ing so sweetly from the woods.

"Tomorrow, I go home," Emilia said suddenly.

"Oh, Emilia Jacalevna," I could tell from her voice
that Helena was sorry now she was cross. "Don't go.
Stay. Only farms are different here. For America this
would be a poor farm—a barren farm—probably the
worst farm anywhere around. We bought the poorest
because it cost the least."

"Iss good farm," Emilia still insisted. "And tomorrow I go home ——"

"Stay," Helena said, "and we can lie in the sun
all day and swim and do all the things people do in
the country. Pick flowers and ——"

"And tomorrow night I be back," Emilia went on.
"But you meeting me this time. You no fooling me."
She laughed to herself. "I'm still remembering you
no meeting me. Wass funny."

So in the morning there was nothing to do but
take her to the six-forty train.

"She'll never come back," Helena was almost crying. "It's all my fault. Probably she's furious and she'll write and make such a polite apology that we'd never know it except that we already do. What do you think?"

"Might she comes back and might she doesn't," I said. "We won't know until we see her."

But we met the evening local anyway and Emilia did get off, loaded down with bundles and two fat shopping bags.

"So," she began as we bumped up the lane, "in New York iss everybody glad you bought a place. Only they say, why you not telling everybody such good kind of news. Comes on Sunday Kosta with Vera he makes you plumbings. Comes Eliko, I told him ask inquiries by his customers for a bathroom. Something rich, I said, black or purple or green something in real American style. Closes the restaurant and comes Anita and Mischa, too, and they have things for you—such things—" She closed her eyes —"Until you see."

We went into the kitchen and I set down her bundles.

"But what you needing now," she said, "I'm giving." She reached down her bodice and unpinned a purse from her underwears and counted out a hundred dollars in bills on the table. "For buying things for planting."

She opened the first parcel. It was a thirty-pound

smoked ham. "For eating when everybody be hungry."

She slit second package. "Such a swinging hammock. See. For resting under the trees after the work is through. And now can begin the farm."

XVI

WHERE SLEEP THE GIANTS STILL

IT LOOKED like we have to have a farm whether we want or not. As soon as Emilia Jacalevna spread the news one our friends Chalvah hurried out as an advance guard to give me notice that eight, ten more were coming on Saturday to stay until we got everything started.

So immediately I heard such news I went to the hardware store to buy the tools we needed.

"Nails, saws, ladders, harrow," Chalvah looked over what I'm picking out. "Even plow, all O.K. Nothing wrong. But if we want to make the work go fast, finish in half the time and enjoy ourselves besides, there's one thing you need most of all. What we always had at home. A good storyteller."

"I know that. But none came in the U.S.A. as far as I ever heard."

"Well, we'll have to stir up our own brains then," Chalvah said. "Think for ourselves stories. Ever you heard, for instance, about the Wolf Who Went to Jerusalem?"

"I heard a hundred time already. But do you know about the Boy Who Built a House from Elephant Bones?"

"No, we don't have that in Khaketi. How it begins?"

So I had the pleasure to recite him all through. Then he told me an anecdote about how his great-great-grandfather made the acquaintance with his great-great-grandmother, a Persian lady. Quite exciting and very romantical.

So by the time the others showed up we had several tales on hand and naturally they remembered some too. So was O.K. everything.

Usually we began telling first thing in morning. Kosta and me, when we work like a good breakfast. Kalbasse sausage snapping hot, new eggs, coupla slices fresh salt cheese, maybe a dish of young cucumbers, and if there's a pan of hot corn bread, besides, we're not gonna say no. Our ladies, specially those from the north, prefer snacks of herring in sour cream over boiled potatoes. As for Besso, he only believes in light food early in day, so we always had for him a special platter of shrimp salad, a few sardines, a little liver paste, or something like. Then Helena Gerbertovna, from California, has the idea that on orange juice runs everything but steam engines, so always a big pitcher of that to get rid of. Well, what with

coffee and hot cream half and half, cake, fruit com-
pote, this and that, it took half the morning to get
through breakfast. And naturally sitting so long at
the table encouraged everybody to start all kinds of
stories.

Of course for his turn Cucule always had to repeat
what he read in college out of books. They don't have
any life to them, those tales. Besides like Dzea Vanno
asked him, "If you read out of books how you know
they're true, those words? You can't see the man in
his eye while he's saying. Maybe they're all made
up."

So with one story and another we pushed the work
along. Our first job was to put on a roof. The old
one had holes so big that every time it rained a water-
fall like Niagara poured down the attic steps, made a
left turn the length of hall, ran down the front stairs
and out the door. Quite an interesting sight to see,
especially inside a house. But not very convenient.

While we were shingling, Piotr—he's got only one
arm and can't do some things—fixed a ladder in the
garret and sat with his head out through the skylight
reciting "The Man in the Panther's Skin," for us to
keep up our spirits. A pretty long poem and it came
out just even with roof.

Afternoons when was too hot for the roof we
painted the frames and shutters and took turns telling.

Abram knew a lot of experiences from the war.
"About the second winter I was on the Turkish

front," was one he told us, "I hadn't seen anybody
from home for over two years. Now, I am first son to
my father and he was still a young man. I heard they
were calling up his age group. I worried where they
gonna send him and how they'll manage at home
when he's gone. Good thing we were working so hard
then that I didn't have more time to think. We were
building hangars, and because the Turks threw so
many bombs out of their airplanes on us we could
only keep on the job at nights.

"Now we got orders to finish up quick and that
night to help us they sent fifty or sixty fellows over
in a truck from a camp on other side of mountains.
We was working all together fast like hell while was
still dark, falling down, running into each other, but
still keeping on.

"But that night the Turks surprised us. Most of
their bombs fell wild but enough were close and
shrapnels got some of our men. How many we didn't
know until daylight, or who.

"And when gray morning came I saw one was my
father, my own father. Dead. And side by side we
was working that whole night through, and I didn't
know. How many times since I asked myself—Maybe
it was him stood next, but one man, to me? When I
carried the plank did he hold the other end? While
we passed bricks was it his hand I touched, there in
the dark? And never I'm gonna know in this world."

"Don't tell no more like that," Chalvah said. "I

painted this same shutter three times over. Tell something cheerful."

"Helena Gerbertovna knows a funny story," I said.
"Her grandmother told it to her. How the World
Almost Ended in St. Johnsbury."

"Don't sound very funny," Chalvah said.

"It is. You go ask her."

Chalvah went in and two seconds he was out like
a bullet, "My God," his teeth chattered so we could
hardly hear him, "My God! Miss Betty sits on the
mantlepiece and Helena Gerbertovna is stabbing at
the wall with a butcher knife."

We all ran in.

"What you doing?" I said.

"Putting in a picture nail," Miss Betty looked
around. "Why?"

Helena Gerbertovna stabbed the wall again. "See,"
she said. "Just what I thought. A plaster partition.
You boys take it down for me and we'll make one
great big room. Six windows and—why are you so
pale?"

But of all the problems on our farm one of the
worst was to get rid of the old chicken coops and pig-
sties and corncribs. Dirty, broken, fallen in, they were
nothing but clubhouses for all the rats in the county.
We pulled them with the tractor; the tractor tipped
over; we tried again; broke our chain. Finally we sat
down disgusted under the apple tree to drink a stone

jug of lemonade our ladies had the kindness to bring us.

"Look," I said, "this is almost the last of our work outside. Altogether we try once more and get it done. Finish up everything. Then tonight I'm gonna tell a story. A story I never told anybody. Gonna be special occasion, needs special story. Knows besides me only three peoples and two is dead. Something different."

In two hours those houses were a pile of stacked boards and we was all cleaned up eating our dinner under the catalpa tree.

"So now begin," everybody told me. Chalvah filled my glass.

"Once on hot, hot day I was about eleven, twelve years old this time, three of my friends and me and my bear, Mischa, we decided we gonna go swimming. Each of us human beings took a piece of corn bread and a little salt in case we had luck to kill a pheasant for *shashlik* with our *shurdules*. Mischa always found some nice treasure of honey for himself or a patch of berries and didn't bother nobody.

"Well, we went up, up, up the mountain farther than ever before until we came to a pocket valley where the Tergie River takes a rest from his racing down just long enough to make little green lake.

"I know the place," Vanno said. "But a landslide filled the whole thing up. While the war was. They sent us there to dig a new opening for water."

"That's the spot, exactly. Well, it was a drier summer than usual this time I'm telling about and the water came lower on rocks, but still it was plenty deep. We had good pleasure to swim and push each other under and play every kind of trick on Mischa we could think. Then we tried dives off a ledge. I went down first and coming up I opened my eyes and I saw a big hole in the cliff. Remember I'm still under the water. I thought to swim in. Maybe it leads up above the water level and I'm gonna hide there and when my friends think I'm drownded and they appreciate me, I'll come back out again and give them a good surprise."

"You didn't have much sense," Cucule said.

"I didn't need much those days. I only had to be smarter than my three dogs and our horse and I got along O.K. Well, when I swam in the hole I saw what shot me out and up to the top in a one second."

"What?"

"Wait! I told the boys. Course they don't believe me. No. No. But maybe they noticed my face was white. My hands, anyway, were shaking.

"So we dived under, all four of us, each went through the hole and swam a little way up in water and came out into—not a room—bigger—a gallery. The size at least of the waiting room in Tiflis railway station. Hollowed out of solid stone in the center of the mountain. And in the half light that leaked through from the cracks in ceiling we saw we found it. Us four little kids, we found it at last."

"What?"

"The Place Where the Giants Came Home To Die."

"Impossible!"

"No, the skulletons was there. Heads. Heads like our heads, only the size of bushel baskets. Great eyeholes our fists would go in. Straight even teeths. The leg bones alone was as tall as any one of us."

"Dishes, swords, money?" Mr. Mockett said, "chests, pots?" Mr. Mockett is one American gentleman, professor, married with a Russian lady.

"Nothing. Only skulletons. What else they had they left outside, I guess, when they came home to die."

"It was cows' heads you saw," Cucule told me.

"Cows' heads, horses' heads were in the fields around Kobiankari by the hundreds. I saw all my life. Every kind of animal skulleton I know from the woods. Fox. Bear. Wolf. These was peoples! Five-fingered hands like us. Long legs. Alive they could have stepped six feet in one stride. I felt sad, especially when I looked at their arms, that I could never see them alive. Alive and wrestling. Must have been a beautiful sight."

"You mean to say," Mr. Mockett asked me, "you mean to say you saw a thing like that and never made notes, never prepared a treatise?"

"Why I should make a treatys?" I said. "I never

had no fight with the giants. I like them. If they be alive sometime, I'm glad to be their friend."

"The giants," Dzea Vanno spoke for the first time. "I heard that tale from old men, who heard from old men. I thought was only gossips. Did it bulge over the forehead, the skull, like they always said?"

"Yes," I told him. "Rounded."

"Horses," Cucule said. "Dead horses."

"Listen. In the war I saw plenty of skulletons. These was men, Cucule. Human beings."

"I can't believe it," Piotr said. "Maybe you made up after landslide to fool peoples."

"How can we fool? We never told anybody. Besides after we started home that day Teddo showed us something. He brought away from the cave the last bone of a little finger. If you don't believe me, go in a Godaouri. Teddo always lived there and as far as I know he's still got the bone."

But even this proof couldn't convince Cucule. "From a dead cow," he said to his wineglass.

Well, before we got in fight fortunately Anita Carlovna remembered a story she knew about another passageway. We went inside to sit around the fireplace so we could roast corn while we listened. And really I think what she told was the best we heard that whole summer.

"Near our village," she began, "was castel stood high on hill. And in this castel was a passageway with steps going down, down, down, nobody knows where, down."

"Why they don't know?" Piotr said.

"Because it's bad luck that passageway. Some people say it goes out to an opening in the cliffs on the seashore. Others think it leads to the old castel owner's dungeon. The reverent says, 'Stay away, maybe in hell it ends?' "

"Well, once on a wedding party everybody was jolly laughing and drinking somehow the talk turns to the old castel. Now the bridegroom likes to show his bride what kind of a brave fellow she had luck to marry with. So he said to the company, 'I'm gonna go down in the passageway my own self alone and everybody that waits me until I come back, I'm gonna bring them nice presents.'

"No, no, he won't hear, no. 'Give me a candle and I'm going.' So the company all went by the opening; the bridegroom buttoned his coat and started down. Step. Step. Step. Fainter and fainter the sound of his feetsteps came back. Step. Step. Well, first two, three hours they laugh, drink, listen for him coming back. Finally they call, holler, shoot guns. Don't come. Days pass. At last only the bride's sitting there alone, hoping, praying. But still he don't come. Ever and ever and ever, don't come."

We were waiting while Anita Carlovna buttered a piece of corn and ate.

"And so then what happened next?" Helena Gerbertovna wanted to know.

"Nothing. He's gone."

"You're not gonna say nobody went after?" Piotr
said. "Impossible!"

"Can't go," Anita told him. "It's bad luck. They
always thought so and now they know for sure."

"Anita Carlovna," Besso said, "eat a piece of corn
and think. Surely you're gonna remember how happened the next part of the story?"

"I be pleased to tell another story," Anita offered,
"but from this one I told all. Isn't any more."

Someway we just couldn't admit to ourselves the
man isn't gonna come out. We asked over and over.
At breakfast, first thing next day Piotr tried again.
"Look, Anita Carlovna, after a coupla years passed
they found the man's bones? Maybe on the seashore,
wasn't it?"

"No."

Miss Betty said, "The man didn't like the young
bride so he made an excuse from this to run away.
Ten years later he comed back and visited the village
with a new wife and ten kids."

"No," Anita Carlovna told her. "The bride waited,
day by day, waited. She was an old lady when I
knew her. Still waiting."

Ten times that day Piotr left our work and came
in and coaxed some more. He couldn't give up.
"Surely a few men, Anita Carlovna, a coupla friends,

at least, went in after him. Maybe they found he died
from heart trouble? Fell over the rocks? Some wild
animal in there ate him?"

But he can't change Anita Carlovna. The man is
gone, gone deep down in the passageway. Forever
gone.

Really if wasn't so far to Europe I think we made a
rescue expedition that very day and went after him
ourselves.

XVII

THE GOOD NEIGHBOR

———

"GOOD mail." Helena Gerbertovna came in from the box one afternoon just as Chalvah and me were ready to sit down to lunch. "Kathleen's coming. She found the chintz. And Emilia Jacalevna and Eliko and Besso and Piotr, they'll start about five on Saturday. And this one is from Uncle John."

I read his words. "He's coming, too," I said.

"And Chancho?"

"I guess."

"You can't live in this place no longer without electricity," Chalvah said all of a sudden. "Got to have electricity." He jumped up and started to tap the walls.

"I lived twenty years in Georgia without it," I said. "And so did you, as far as that goes."

"You didn't have no American ladies visiting you there," Chalvah said. "Entirely different situation now. What Helena Gerbertovna's friends think when they come and find you keeping her in place without the electric? What kind impression that gives of Georgians?"

"I don't know how to make the wires," I told him.

"I show you."

"But after this you can only come out on Sundays."

"I start everything now. Then I draw you pictures on the walls how goes the wires and where the connections come and you be working on that until I come the next week. Then I make you more pictures again."

"I don't know," Helena Gerbertovna poured him coffee. "Are you sure? ——"

"Don't worry," Chalvah said. "I know ladies is very particular, but you gonna paint the walls anyway, so whatever marks I make won't show."

"I mean wouldn't it short-circuit us when we turned on the bathtub or something," Helena Gerbertovna asked.

"Certainly not." Chalvah refused the cream to show he's offended. "But if you don't trust me ——"

No. No. We said we had full confidence in him. So we went down and got the cables and the switches and the tape and all the things he needed and the same time we stopped at the station to meet Helena's friend, Kathleen Patrickovna.

"I have something wonderful," she said soon as she got in the door. "For you, George. And I made it myself. Boilo."

"Boilo? Sounds like a bleach." Helena Gerbertovna said, " 'Boilo washes briter.' "

Kathleen Patrickovna opened her suitcase and took out a bottle full of honey-colored something. "Boilo. It's a drink. Wonderful."

"Well, let's try," I said.

"Certainly." Chalvah got a corkscrew. "What can we lose but our health?"

"Fill up the glasses first with cracked ice," Kathleen said, "And after pour enough Boilo in to come to the top."

Chalvah like a brave man took the first sip. "Excellent. I kiss the hands that made it." He gave a bow to Kathleen.

I tried a sip. Really was something interesting. Smooth as cream and with a faraway taste—like orange blossoms smell. "What's in it?"

"Luscious," Helena said. We had another all around. "Let's save a glass for the others tonight."

"No. I'll make some more this afternoon," Kathleen said. "It's easy. You take three oranges and a lemon and you chop them fine and roll them in honey. Do you have a percolator?"

"Yes."

"Then you put the chopped fruit in where the coffee grounds would go ——"

"Yes?"

"And you fill the pot up with corn whisky, plug it in and let it perk."

"My God!" Chalvah said.

"And when it's done you strain it and let it get cold and that's Boilo. Who's coming tonight?"

"A lot of the Georgians."

"What are the neighbors around here like?"

"Didn't any come to see us yet," I said.

"Stop worrying about it," Helena told me.

"But I like to be good friends to my neighbors."

"Boilo," Chalvah said to himself. "My God!"

"Nobody that knows anything comes to call until you have your curtains up," Helena Gerbertovna said. "That means you've got the cake ready and the lemons sliced thin ——"

"How DO you do," Kathleen shook hands with the air. "But a pleasure."

"Is this a general rule," I said, "or is it one that you made up?"

"No," Helena said. "This time it's true. Isn't it. Kathy?"

"Let's have another glass of Boilo," Kathleen said. "And next time I'm going to try how it comes out with tangerines and a grapefruit."

But it seems like Mrs. Cleevendon, the lady from the big place two farms over, and Helena Gerbertovna wasn't running on the same track at all because the next Sunday, the hottest day in sixty-seven years, she came visiting. Not only curtains wasn't up; neither was the ceiling.

I was in my swimming trunks working in the living

room feeding cable up through the beams to Chalvah.
I heard a knock. I heard a voice introducing itself.
My God! A lady! And I'm over seventy-five percent
naked. I dropped the cable and stepped into the
nearest place handy. Happened to be an old grampa
clock Helena Gerbertovna bought at an auction few
weeks before.

Besso escorted in a lady. "Be pleased to take a seat,"
he said. "For the moment our hostess is absent walking in the woods. But I call her." I could see them
through a crack. He went to the table and poured a
small glass of sherry and brought a plate of crackers.
"You will do my friend the honor," he said, "to drink
this little glass and I hope he often has the pleasure
to see you in his house."

"I thank you," Mrs. Cleevendon said, "but I do not
indulge."

"Excuse me just a minute." Besso edged toward
door. "I don't speak English so good. But the friend
of our hostess is here. I call her." He went in the hall.
"Kathleen Patrickovna?"

"What do you want, Besso?" she answered from
the kitchen. "I'm terribly busy."

"Guest."

"Oh. Right away."

Besso closed the door and had the sense to stay on
the other side of it.

All this time Chalvah keeps pulling up lengths of

cable. "Not the end yet, Giorgi?" he calls. I hear the cable sliding across the floor. "End?"

I'm quiet in my clock like a mouse.

Chalvah crawls through the hole in the upstairs floor and starts working himself across the living room beams. "Giorgi?"

He's about out to his waist and true he didn't have no clothes on so far, but there was no need for Mrs. Cleevendon to scream. She ought to have known the pants was coming.

"Oh," Chalvah said. He's laying between the ceiling beams. "I beg your pardon. You wasn't who I expected to see. I mean I'll call somebody." He started to slide back. "Please be so kind to take a chair. You'll have to excuse me, I can't offer you any refreshments. If you please help yourself to a glass of wine. On the table."

"Thank you," Mrs. Cleevendon said. "I do not take spirits. I wear the white ribbon. Band of Hope."

"Well," Chalvah said philosophically, "In this world if we don't got hope what do we got? Be so kind to pour a glass and whatever you hope is I give myself the pleasure to wish you have it."

Helena Gerbertovna came in. At last. They began to have lady conversation. Maybe is gonna be O.K. everything, I thought to myself. Only too bad they don't make clocks with a place to sit down.

Mrs. Cleevendon was describing her antiques.

"—Luster pitcher for a dollar," Helena said.

"I paid thirty cents for mine."

"—And a cherry cupboard."

"If it's the original hardware?" Mrs. Cleevendon said. "And your clock?"

"—is signed inside." Helena came across the room and threw open the door.

"How do you do," I said. I came out. "Happened as I was going swimming I noticed this clock was running slow. About five minutes. Little adjustment. Be all right."

Helena Gerbertovna made introductions.

"Oh," Mrs. Cleevendon said soon she heard our name. "You would seem to be—"she gave little cough like people do before they say a dirty word—"foreigners. Are you Russian?"

"I'm a Georgian, madame."

"Oh. Then you must be a prince. They all seem to be princes."

"No, madame. My father was a peasant."

"You're too modest, I'm sure. One never hears of anything but princes."

"And my great-grandfather was a peasant." I said. "And before that my great-great-grandfather. As a matter of fact we go straight back to Noah."

"To Noah?"

"He landed on Arrarat. I guess you read that. Later on he moved where we live now. Drier location."

"Oh." she said. "I see. Noah. Well. And now

tell me," she went on, "do you like this little place?"

We said we did. Helena began to describe what we were doing and I made excuse to get upstairs and put my clothes on. When I came down again Helena was just taking Mrs. Cleevendon into the dining room. I went after them. Table is all set and cake is on the plates and coffeepot makes happy bubbling. "How nice of Kathy," Helena Gerbertovna said "Everything ready. Will you sit here, Mrs. Cleevendon?"

But must be Helena Gerbertovna was more nervous then she looked. Otherwise before she poured Mrs. Cleevendon a steaming hot cup of corn whisky she would have noticed Kathy was making Boilo.

Mrs. Cleevendon turned green. "I'm afraid," she said, "I must go." She got up. "I— I must be somewhere. Another time—." She gathered her gloves.

We had to follow her to the door. "I'm sorry you can't stay," I said, "but please come again. And next time I hope to have pleasure to meet your husband."

"I lost Mr. Cleevendon three years ago."

"I'm very sorry," I said "I hope you find again." In my experience husbands that get lost usually do it on purpose, but I had to say something cheerful.

"Good-by. Good-by."

Helena could hardly wait for her to get in the car. "He's dead, her husband. My God! You hope she finds again."

Kathy rolled out the swing where she was hiding herself. "I'm glad that's over," she said.

"Why you don't tell me?" I told them. "Why you don't say a widow?"

"The old—," Kathy kicked the trellis.

"I'll have the same," Helena said.

"Easy for you girls to talk," I said. "Suppose you be left to fight the world alone, you be worse than her." I ran out to car.

She was just pulling out. "Excuse me," I put my head through the window. "I didn't know you was a widow. What day you like me to come and bring in your wood?"

"Wood?"

"Or if somebody has that duty, to plow? Whatever you need."

"Plow?"

"Excuse me. I don't know just how you make the arrangements here. I never lived on farm before. We have habit to work for widows one regular day, but if you have some other system," I said, "I be glad to do my share, however it comes."

"Why, thank you. Thank you very much." I see she can even smile, a thing I would never have suspected. "But so far I can manage. By the way, would you and your wife be free to have dinner with me one day next week?"

So we went and after we got to be good friends and good neighbors to each other and we used to visit often. And once after we knew each other a long, long time she said to me, "You know I didn't quite understand you first day we met I——"

"Perfectly all right, Mrs. Cleevendon," I said. "Don't apologize. You thought we was drunkards and we thought you was the crossest patch we ever saw. After all, everybody can make mistakes."

XVIII

THE GROUND KNOWS

─────

During all this time, since I was in Virginia, I imported a kind of chemical from Germany that I made into an ink used on duplicating machines. Probably I would be an old man still selling this only I didn't agree with the things that began to happen in Germany.

So now how could I send my money to buy the chemicals any more—and still keep a clear conscience? I tried to persuade myself what difference does my few pennies make? I'm only one man. What's one man? But then my common sense told me—one man is one man. Without the leaf there would never be the forest.

So I must look for another way to earn my living. I decided to farm.

First thing I found out is that one of the best ways to make money on a farm is by not raising chickens. But it cost me a thousand dollars and took me a year to find this out. A very unsocial animal, chickens, picking each other to death. And stupid besides. Flopping and fluttering, creating commotions, they practically invite foxes and dogs and skunks and weasels to chase them.

"Believe me," I said to Helena Gerbertovna the day we sold the last coopful, "I'm through with chickens. And when I go back in Kobiankari maybe I convince them about subways and the radio; maybe I persuade them to the Empire State Building and Automats but they never gonna believe that in America chickens has to wear spectacles and tin skirts so they don't eat each other up. Never in this world."

Well after chickens I tried goats. Why people don't try to understand goats? They have silky coats and gentle mouths and the daintiest appetite can be—a special weed here, patch of sweet grass there, few pear tree leaves for appetizer; a crunch of bitter stalk; a snuffle at the clover blossoms—they pick like meadow was a cafeteria counter. Besides they give milk that's all cream. What more could a person want? But you can't get nobody to buy their milk or the good cheese from it neither. All have prejudices. "Goats smell." Ridiculous. They don't smell half as much as people.

So next I tried bees, then corn and after that sheep and grain and pigs and flax. I was working right through the farm bulletins and pretty soon almost nothing be left except Drying Fruit for the Export

Market and Raising Peafowl for Pin-Money and Pleasure.

Something is wrong someplace. But what? Can't be the farm, all good rich ground with nice slope to the creek. So must be me, myself. Maybe I didn't work hard enough. Maybe from my life in America I fell into the habit of expecting my piece of bread always gonna come the easy way. Some things you can fool by giving half your work, but never the ground. The ground knows, and now my ground was insulted at me.

So I made my mind to try again and this time to plow my whole self into my furrows; to plant my very best work with the seed.

But what to try? I was thinking over one thing and another. Then in early spring I heard men at the feed house talking about crops and my neighbor, Mr Glidden, said, "Tomatoes. Big money in tomatoes. I paid my mortgage and put on a new roof. I even dug a cess pool. All with tomatoes."

That interested me. "How you selling them?"

"Can company buys," one man told me.

"Can company?"

"Soup company," Mr. Glidden said. "But I don't sell to them. I sell on the market in Dock Street. First of the season I get maybe a dollar or even a dollar fifty a basket and on down until the end I get a quarter a carrier from the Eyetalian folks for ketch."

"Ketch?"

"Ketchup. What you eat on fried potatoes."

"Gonna be tomatoes for me," I told Helena Gerbertovna that night. "A beautiful fruit. With personality. Something to enjoy with your eyes and your mouth while you working."

In the middle of March we sent our order to the seed company and they started the plants and by May when we drove to Jersey to get them, they were fifteen to twenty inches high and some had even set little tomatoes.

I had the field ready and Mr. Glidden showed me how to plant. We made ourselves dibbles, heavy curved sticks with a brass nose and we poked a hole with this, set the plant in, tamped the ground down around it and ladled some water out of our bucket and then on to the next one.

After a few hours had a kind of dance to it like a ballet. Poke, set, tamp and splash. Poke, set, tamp and splash.

Plants catched hold good and I cultivated and cross-cultivated until my field was a smooth brown velvet carpet and if green tip of a weed dared to show himself—I took for personal insult.

In July I got my first load off, forty baskets, and I took to Dock Street and stayed all night on the market and I sold for one dollar a basket. Was O.K.

But next week prices dropped and same time tomatoes started ripening so fast I had to get a fellow to help me with the picking so I could pack.

This packing was most important part. "Always put the best ones on the bottom," Mr. Glidden told me the day I made up my first load, "and you'll keep your customers long as you got the strength to plant."

And he took a whole afternoon off just show us how to do the restaurant baskets. First a circle of green tomatoes at the bottom with a good fat one to fill the center. Then another row on top of that. You build it around and around as you go up. Dark green, pale green, faint pink, coral, rosy red, scarlet. Two top layers must be dead ripe so as the cook uses the basket down the lower part gets ready. Quite an art.

About third week in August peak crop started coming in. No time to wait on Dock Street now to catch the best price. Had to hurry home get another load off. Back to the market. Home. Market. I was lucky if I got to bed four nights in seven, and at the table I dozed with fork halfway between my mouth and the plate. Faster. Faster.

But I was gonna keep it up. Keep it up if it killed me. I gonna prove to my ground I'm good enough to be its owner. I wasn't a human being no more. I was a machine. A tomato harvester. Automatic. Self-adjusting. Works in all weathers. Pick, pack, lift and carry, Pick, pack, lift, carry. Pick, pack—Turn the lever and it will swing and load. Swing and load. And all the time the sun pounded down hotter and hotter. When I wiped the sweat off I wiped the pollen in—made me look like I was corroding.

On August twenty-seventh we took off three hundred and twelve baskets. So many, there was nothing to do but give them to a commission house so I could get back to start picking again.

"He sends us a check in three or four days," I told Helena Gerbertovna when I got home. "Least we get thirty-seven cents. Market is holding good."

But that night a storm blew up and hail rattled at the windows and after began a thick steady rain, all through the next day and the next. Couldn't get in the fields at all. Solid glue. Then Sunday a blazing sun came up and by noon we knew the worst. Our last tomatoes was off. What was left was stewing in a six acre cook pot. Finished.

"Well," I said, soon as I made up my mind to it, "that's nobody's fault and it could be worse. Our first loads paid most of the expenses and what commission man sends us will take care of fertilizer and be our profit. This time I think everything be O.K."

Two days while I watched for mail man I told Helena what we gonna buy with our money and at last envelope came. I opened. There was the check. I bringed it in proudly.

"$55.75," Helen read it. "There's some mistake."

"$55.75! Can't be," I said.

She pulled out a slip. "163 baskets at thirty-eight cents—$61.94 less 10 per cent, net $55.75. 149 baskets dumped."

"Dumped," I said.

"Dumped," Helena was looking at slip.

"They can't do that." I looked paper over on both sides.

"But they did." Helena went and looked out window at our field. "They did. They can do anything."

My heart was bleeding. Not even to let me know so I could come and give them away to hungry people on the street. Dumped. My tomatoes at the bottom of the river in Philadelphia, maybe still round, still red, still satiny to the hand's touch—my tomatoes lying in the mud under the slow-running current. Wasted. My work throwed back at me.

Maybe that be life for somebody. Not for me. I got a job.

But often and often I'm still thinking and still I don't convince myself. Can't be such a thing as a man with land and his own two good hands can't earn his bread on a farm. Impossible? Because if that be so then how we started our world from the beginning. No. Is some other reason.

But what?

XIX

UNCLE JOHN NEVER DIES

To HAVE a forest ready for our old age we were planting trees on the farm, thousands of trees the size of
twigs. Spruces like Christmas greens and pines where
the thrushes could sit to sing, and birches, because
birches look so happy always while they're growing.

In the middle of our work the mail carrier honked
us twice from the gate to say: A telegram.

It was from Emilia Jacalevna:

I GREET YOU WITH LOVE AND KISSES TO GIVE
SAD NEWS. PLEASE COME ON THE FUNERAL.
UNCLE JOHN IS DEAD.

Dzea Vanno dead!

All the joy tipped out from our hearts and for us,
that day, the sun didn't shine any more.

Dzea Vanno dead? It left an empty hole in my life.
Who will talk to me now about the old days at home?
Who will care about our village? Who remember the
time we hid Petro from the soldier, the tricks good

Bootsa Boy could do, or the day I took first prize for my ornamental scabbard design? Who will laugh if I tell again about the chief of police when he got so drunk he sleeped in the pigs' house instead of his own?

Nobody. Nobody to sit around the table with me and drink for friends only us two ever knew. Nobody to bring me all his ends and odds for fixing, broken meat slicer, electric sign that don't work, phonograph with the spring gone, bargain meat grinder. Nobody left even to call me Bijo Gogio. It was more than Uncle John that was gone. Part of home died with him.

He had a big funeral. I think he been pleased himself to see it. All around where his coffin was set, in the center of the church, flowers bloomed like a garden. Roses, lilies in the valley, carnations, jonquils, hyacinths, a crushed bouquet of violets some little kid came up and dropped. I never saw him before, but Uncle John was something to him, too.

Besso passed, giving out the candles for us to hold and one by one they were lighted. Must have been over three hundred people there. I saw two from Pittsburgh and one clear from Virginia. And all the while the priest chanted and the music made its sad answerings, I thought about the last time I saw Dzea Vanno just a coupla weeks before.

He kept a little restaurant on Fourth Street after he came from California, but one morning he got tired to have it any longer so that day he sold a half interest in the place to six, seven Russians. Night they came, all in same hour, each with a lawyer, to take ownership. First was a mixup but at last they got settled among selves and paid Uncle John's money over.

"First," he told me, "I'm gonna put on a side 'nough to buy best leg can find for Igor Andrevitch. Let he have enjoyment to dance again. And then we take Chancho and go on Orchard Street and with rest of the money we find presents for our friends."

First he thought to buy whole pushcart full with gloves—all sizes, all kinds. "See," he said, "we roll on the street. Go from friend's house to friend's house. They come on out and choose gloves how many can use. With our best compliments. Makes a nice joke. What you think?"

But we couldn't persuade man to sell us cart.

"O.K. I'm gonna choose presents only for lady friends anyway," Dzea decided. "For the men I'll have a party instead."

So for almost two hours we had good time to look along in windows until Dzea Vanno saw something catched his taste in a basement shop.

"Garters," he asked clerk inside. "Like in window. The painted ones or those with oyster's feathers on. Something rich."

Man showed box full all kinds.

Dzea chosed from red satin a pair. "How much?"

"Twelve dollars a gross."

"What means gross?"

"Hundred forty-four pairs."

"I take," Dzea Vanno said. "I don't know quite so many ladies yet, but I'm certainly gonna make more acquaintance all time."

About this I don't doubt he was one hundred per cent right. Because when he came in U.S.A. Uncle John was speaking Russian, Turkish, Persian, Syrian, Armenian, Tartar, and Georgian. Naturally, it didn't leave much place in his head for this language. So every time he couldn't think of a word he needed in English he just said, "I luff you." He surely made lots of new friends this way, specially lady friends.

On the way out from shop Dzea Vanno had an idea. "Look," he told the man, "I want you to buy me so many as garters, the same many little silver bells, and sew on the buckles. The ladies gonna ting-aling-a-ling-a-ling when they walking. Be something different."

"Cost you a fortune," the man said. "Labor alone ———"

Dzea Vanno gave him a bill. "Never mind the expense. I pay. And remember, boy," he said to me, "when you giving a present, always giving something rich or don't giving at all."

How could man like Uncle John be dead? Man who loved so deep the world. Man who made such friend of life. But he was dead, and now the censer swung and incense rose and after they spoke the praising words. But Uncle John didn't need them. What good he did was wrote on the faces around his casket, was weighed in the shining tears that caught the candlelight and turned to diamonds.

Poor Chancho, he stood at the back until they laid the ribbon across Dzea's brow, and then he came not once but again and again to kiss it.

I took his arm. "Let's we go by the side a minute," I said. "So many of Dzea's friends here ———"

"Giorgi Ivanitch," poor fellow, his words almost choked him, "Uncle John left me. Why he left me?"

"Everybody has to die, Chancho."

"I made him mad. Lots of time. But I didn't mean it. He knew I didn't mean it."

"He knew, Chancho."

"They said I was crazy. All the people. The boys threw stones at me. But Uncle John knew I wasn't. World was made for us all. He said so."

"That's right."

"Uncle John! Uncle John!"

"Don't, Chancho," I said. "He can't answer you no more. You only gonna make the other people feel bad."

"If Uncle John be dead, they throw stones at me again."

"No, Chancho," I said. "You can come home with me if you want. World was made for us all, I guess. But only few men, men like Dzea, ever want to believe it."

All too soon that dark wet day we stood in the cemetery at the grave's edge and while we listened to the priest a cold hand was knocking on my heart. And each time I raised eyes from the spaded earth I saw my own fear, given back like from a mirror, on the face of every man beside me. Eliko, Arsenna, Kosta, they was thinking, too, as they threw the clod, Who be next? Maybe I'm the one—to die so far from home—to lie in stranger dirt, to be only name written in letters nobody can read?

On the way back we couldn't say a word, no one of us.

In Arto's was the funeral party this time, but before we could begin first Zachara and Besso who wasn't speaking together almost three years must settle their quarrel and even I had to be friends again to Cucule and both we forget what happened, all for Uncle John's remembry. Is good this, even if an old-time way. It lets a man be sure he will finish from the grave, at least, what he has a duty to work for through his whole life—bring peace among his friends.

So twenty men we sat down around the table to drink toasts for Dzea Vanno and eat for him *shilah p'lavi*, the Meal For the Day of Death. Rice, it is, with enough pieces of fatted young lamb in and salt and black, black pepper, and onions, and thyme all cooked together until it turns velvet smooth. Hot and rich. Special good for people that is cold from new-turned ground, empty with looking at open graves.

But we didn't fill the glasses only for Uncle John this day. We remembered other men, too, that left our table. Davit and how every year he went to such troubles and strunged nuts on strings for dipping in thickened grape juice—all to make *chuchkella* so little kids born here would know what candy tasted like at home.

A toast for Papa, too, who hunted thirty years to find somebody could speak our language and never thought his time was wasted.

Yes, and Nick, and Vasso, and Petri, many others, we remembered them, every one.

And somehow the table did what all the words couldn't—gave us back ourselves and made us a promise that so long as one of our friends sits down to take pleasure in food and company and wine so long, too, we shall never be forgotten. More than that no man can want.

And so like everything in this world must, it came to an end our party, and Eliko rose for the last toast. To Dzea Vanno.

"I drink this little glass," he said, "for man who had the good sense don't leave us no fortune to fight over. He leaved us instead his responsibilities and his pleasures, too, with a good example how to enjoy them. Still lots and lots left to do in this world yet. So priest gonna excuse me, I'm sure, if a little I change the Bible words he read on the cemetery and say different way. In the midst of death still we are in a life. Amen."

XX

ON EASTER DAY

———

As soon we came out of the bank I said to Helena Gerbertovna "And now let's have a party."

"What for this time?"

"Because now I paid the mortgage all. Why, I really own a piece of America."

"Good as any other reason," Helena Gerbertovna said. "Who we have and when?"

"Easter and we ask everybody. All the Georgians and all our American friends, too. I like to have a really big party. So big that for the next ten years people remember everything did it happen Before or did it happen After our party."

"What was the best party we ever went to?" Helena Gerbertovna asked me.

"Hard to decide." I was thinking. "Maybe when Besso's daughter got married and they had the musicians for three days and platters of fresh hot corn bread every meal. That was pretty good. What you chose?"

"Time at Eliko's. Was it Christmas or Easter?"

"Easter how I remember it. And Vasso was *tamada* that time to lead the table and give all the toast. And he made such a nice speech. After he drank for everybody in turn, somebody proposed a glass for him— 'for the man who did so much for his country' and he said, 'I thank you for your words but whatever I did for my country was not smallest part of what my country did for me.' A good said answer."

"The thing I remember," Helena said, "was that we sat down at the table about two o'clock and first we had *zakuski* of fishes and salads and what all and in two hours the table was a mess. Emilia cleared everything and started with a new tablecloth and chickens and a ham—she had six new tablecloths before the night was over and by the last one she had started on her linen sheets.

"I think I see if I can negotiate a small pig for our party and we roast whole outdoors on a spit."

"I'm going to make everything I can think of. Every single thing."

"And plenty of it," I said.

So we sent invitations and Saturday before Easter seventeen peoples turned up and with four little kids and us made twenty-three. "Nice comfortable size for a party," I told Helena.

I was right. About four o'clock we sat down and we was just enough to make a good table. Everybody enjoyed themselves to eat and drink and we sang all our Georgian songs and our American friends gave nice tunes for reply—about some house they used to live in before in Kentucky and a lady that went around on her knees carrying a banjo and cowboys who had troubles and all the college songs—some of the best songs in America, I noticed, is the college ones, especially about football. Must be a very musical game to watch, that.

One of our ladies, Vera Petrovna, is Estonian and someway they found out Estonian birthday greeting is same tune as California University hymn and so they had fine time singing and singing, each their own words—quite like a duet, when they had luck to come out even.

Yes, we was a pretty good company and once I made excuse to leave the table and go outside just so I could catch it all in my heart to keep—the voices floating away through the trees, the feathers of smoke rising from the chimney, the roasting baking buttery smell sifting out of the kitchen door, the windows shining with golden light—people being happy in my house.

They was still singing when I came back—"What leaves a man when he rides to war?" Piotr's big bass asked. "He leaves a wife so true," Besso's sweet tenor answered. And then the company in chorus, "Such leaves a man when he rides to war."

"I gonna drink last glass now," Piotr, our *tamada*, said when song was finished, "is only eleven o'clock, but tomorrow be Easter and we want to keep some appetite."

Next morning, in honor of the Day, all us foreigners have habit to kiss each other and say, *"Christos Voskrecè."*

"Looks so nice," Miss Betty says, she's giving childrens their breakfast, "What does it mean?"

"Means Christ rose. You supposed to answer, *'Voistinu Voskrecè.'* I do believe that He rose! Like Americans say, 'Happy Easter.'"

"But much better," Miss Betty said, "Christ rose. I like it. Sounds so sweet and serious for Easter morning. Christ rose."

"Christ rose!" Besso came in the kitchen and kissed everybody.

"I believe—how you say—I believe He rose?" Miss Betty told him, "But I thought you was an atheist, Besso?"

"Certainly I am. We take for example story of Adam and Eva ——"

"I know," Miss Betty said. "You explained me that yesterday. But why you say, Christ rose?"

"Why? After all," Besso looked hurt, "just because person is atheist—*Christos Voskrecè,* Piotr. Challico—" He kissed them on both cheeks as they came through the door.—"Because person is atheist he don't need to have bad manners. Who likes to crack Easter egg with me?"

Childrens all gathered around him. "Me. Me."

"I can't do nothing unless you find egg with your own name," he said. "Otherwise wouldn't be official. Now you found? We gonna tap ends of eggs together —so. See, I hold and you hit. One whose egg gets cracked loses. Pays a forfeit. But won't be me. No. No. Never be Besso. All right. Ready? Smack. What? Mine broke. Now how happened that? I try another."

Little kids kept jumping up and down, "Me next. Me next." Everyone they broke Besso's eggs. He found four presents in his pocket and lined them up. "Funny," he said, "everybody wins from me. Giorgi Ivanitch, next Easter I want you to carve me a stone egg. I gonna color it—blue, I think, and paint regular designs on and I win from everybody. But don't tell—" he whispers to childrens, "—if you don't say a word——"

They all closed mouths up tight. No. No. No. No. All four heads shaking.

"—Why I take you for my partners."

After breakfast we made a fire and let it die to bright embers, then we stuck two forked branches either side, spitted the pig, laid it across and then turned around and around while it grew crickling, crackling browner and browner and the dogs sat on their haunches and watched with hungry eyes and long tongues and so, too, did the peoples.

Challico was *tamada* for the table this day and he made a good one—kept the songs going and the glasses filled and said the toasts in words that didn't stop at your ears but went straight through to the heart. "Give me attention," he said at last. "We drank lotta toasts today—for everybody as himself, for the childrens, for the mothers and the fathers, for our hostess and our host. Now I gonna propose for something different. Piotr, please to stop cracking nuts and listen me."

"With pleasure," Piotr said, "I only wish I had donkey's ears so I could hear you better. My glass is empty, what's more."

Somebody filled his glass. He held to light. "Very beautiful wine this, looks like melted rubies. I hope you making beautiful toast to go with it, Challico."

"Before I was interrupted," Challico went on, "I said we was gonna drink for something different. Well this little glass is for Home. I see lotta American faces around me. I like to tell them we pleased to see them at our party especially since we had honor to be at their wide table, which is United States in America, for a long time and enjoy all the things they put before us. We tried to be good guests. I hope we was. That's one Home. Lotsa other kind of peoples we are here, too. Georgians, Russians, Greek, Latvian, Estonian, Irish—regular League a Nations. I drink for all those Homes, too, and it gives me hope when I see us sitting down so peaceful together, maybe whole world gonna learn how to do it, too. After all it's only enjoyable way to live. So—for Home."

"I drink with pleasure," I said. "For Home. Its floor is the earth; its roof is the sky."